Literature Circles Resource Guide

Teaching Suggestions, Forms,
Sample Book Lists, and Database

Literature Circles Resource Guide

Teaching Suggestions, Forms, Sample Book Lists, and Database

Bonnie Campbell Hill
Katherine L. Schlick Noe
Nancy J. Johnson

Christopher-Gordon Publishers, Inc.
Norwood, Massachusetts

Credits

Response Journal Rubric used with permission of Emile Hard, Tahoma School District.

Form adapted from *Literacy Assessment: A Handbook of Instruments* (Rhodes 1993), used with permission of Lynn K. Rhodes.

Presentation Rubric used with permission of Trilby Cohen, Heidi Hanson, and Melissa Sargent from *Classroom Based Assessment*.

Every effort has been made to contact copyright holders for permission to reproduce borrowed material where necessary. We apologize for any oversights and would be happy to rectify them in future printings.

Copyright © 2001 by Christopher-Gordon Publishers, Inc.

Christopher-Gordon Publishers, Inc.
1502 Providence Highway, Suite 12
Norwood, MA 02062
(800) 934-8322

Printed in the United States of America

10 9 8 7 6 5 4 3 2   05 04 03 02 01

Library of Congress Catalogue Number: 00-109248
ISBN: 1-929024-23-1

Short Contents

Section 1
Teaching Suggestions and Forms   1

Section 2
Sample Book Lists   97

Section 3
Bibliography of Professional Resources for Literature Circles   167

About the Authors   175

Expanded Contents

Section 2
Sample Book Lists   97

Section 3
Bibliography of Professional Resources for Literature Circles   167

About the Authors   175

Acknowledgments

We want to thank Sue Canavan from Christopher-Gordon for her generous support and encouragement on this newest literature circles project. We also appreciate the feedback from our reviewers. We offer a special thank you to our families, specifically to Laura Hill for her help as a reviewer. Finally, this project would not have been possible without the computer expertise and countless hours contributed by Steve Hill and Lynne Schueler. We also want to thank the following teachers who generously shared their forms and booklists for this Resource Guide:

Sue Elvrum and Linda Johnson, Kindergarten, Brighton School, Lynnwood, Washington.

Christy Clausen, First Grade/Reading Specialist, East Ridge Elementary, Woodinville, Washington.

Margee Morfitt, First/Second Grade, South Whidbey Primary, Whidbey Island, Washington.

Vicki Yousoofian, First Grade, Yokohama International School, Yokohama, Japan.

Holly Dietrich, Multiage Primary, Cedar Valley Elementary, Lynnwood, Washington.

Diana Kastner and Ann Gutleber, First Grade, Brighton School, Lynnwood, Washington.

Megan Sloan, First/Second Grade, Cathcart Elementary, Snohomish, Washington.

Lisa Norwick, Second Grade, Brookside/Cranbrook School, Bloomfield Hills, Michigan.

Elizabeth Bentley, Second Grade, Student Teacher, North City Elementary, Shoreline, Washington.

Lisa Woodbury, Second Grade, Orting Elementary, Orting, Washington.

Sandy Figel and Donna Kerns, Second Grade, Brighton School, Lynnwood, Washington.

Trilby Cohen, Heidi Hanson, and Melissa Sargent, Primary Grades, Syre Elementary, Shoreline, Washington.

Cindy Flegenheimer and Linda Horn, Third Grade, Brighton School, Lynnwood, Washington.

Mary Lou Laprade, Third Grade, John Hay Elementary, Seattle, Washington.

Lori Scobie, Third/Fourth Grade, North City Elementary, Shoreline, Washington.

Emilie Hard, Fourth/Fifth Grade/Principal, Tahoma School District, Tahoma, Washington.

Barry Hoonan, Multiage Intermediate, Odyssey Multiage Program, Bainbridge Island, Washington.

Anne Klein, Fourth/Fifth Grade, Seaview Elementary, Edmonds, Washington.

Sarah Dunkin, Fourth/Fifth Grade, Chehalem Elementary, Beaverton, Oregon.

Kathleen Armstrong, Fifth Grade, Mary Institute and St. Louis Country Day School, St. Louis, Missouri.

Kirstin Gerhold, Fifth Grade, Columbia Elementary, Mukilteo, Washington.

Kary Brown, Fifth Grade, Brighton School, Lynnwood, Washington.

Judy Kendall and Joyce Foster, Sixth Grade, Mary Institute and St. Louis Country Day School, St. Louis, Missouri.

Janine King, Sixth/Seventh/Eighth Grade, Brighton School, Lynnwood, Washington.

Book Overview

Section 1   Teaching Suggestions and Forms

Classroom-tested, teacher-developed guidelines and forms for four components of literature circles: Organization, Discussion, Written Response, and Extension Projects. A fifth section, Families and Literature Circles, includes ideas for involving families in the classroom, as well as ways to invite families to share books at home.

In each section, you will find a brief introduction with several teaching suggestions. The forms designated with a border can be used for instructional planning or enlarged for charts in your classroom. In the remainder of each section, we include forms for students to use as they discuss, write, and respond to literature. You can easily adapt the charts and forms on the CD-ROM to meet the needs of your particular group of students and literature circle organization.

Section 2.   Sample Book Lists

Lists of books organized by topic, theme, genre, or author at varying grade levels, primary through middle school. These books have been recommended by teachers who have used them in their classrooms. They represent both familiar books, as well as more recent titles.

Section 3.   Bibliography of Professional Resources for Literature Circles

Comprehensive list of professional books and web sites for literature circles. This section also contains a description of a web site for literature circles developed by Katherine L. Schlick Noe of Seattle University (http://fac-staff.seattleu.edu/kschlnoe/LitCircles). The web site includes supplementary information on literature circles and email connections with teachers who are using literature circles in their classrooms.

CD-ROM

1. *Teaching Suggestions and Forms*—The charts and forms provided in this resource guide are also included on the CD-ROM, formatted for both Mac and PC use. With the CD-ROM, it is easy to modify the forms to fit your needs.

2. *Book Lists*—Sample Book Lists are also included on the CD-ROM.

3. *Database of Children's and Young Adult Literature*—All of the books in the book lists are also included in the database, along with a brief annotation. You can search the database by title, author, illustrator, theme, genre, publisher, or year of publication. You can add to or delete titles from the database to create a customized list of excellent books for literature circles.

4. *Literature Circles References and Resource Center Web Site* (http://fac-staff.seattleu.edu/kschlnoe/LitCircles)—A link to this web site is included on the CD-ROM.

Introduction

The *Literature Circles Resource Guide* provides the practical support you need to make literature circles succeed. The information provided in this guide should answer the kinds of questions you ask colleagues: "How did you get students to think about their book before their discussion?" "Do you have a copy of a planning form for extension projects?" "What books can I use for a theme on friendship for my third graders?"

This resource guide is not intended to stand alone. It is designed to supplement and extend two professional books on literature circles: *Getting Started with Literature Circles*, by Katherine L. Schlick Noe and Nancy J. Johnson (1999); and *Literature Circles and Response*, edited by Bonnie Campbell Hill, Nancy J. Johnson and Katherine L. Schlick Noe (1995). These books provide the rationale and underlying philosophy, as well as detailed explanations and strategies for teaching and assessing all elements of literature circles (e.g., how to teach discussion strategies, how to develop students' written response, and how to extend response through the arts). Many of the forms in this resource guide are from these professional books. Explanations of specific forms can be found in the book referenced at the bottom of each page. Some of the assessment forms are also published in *Classroom Based Assessment* (Hill, Ruptic, and Norwick, 1998).

The notebook of resources includes sample forms that teachers have developed for their students. We hope that these samples spark new ideas rather than limit you. The best form is often a blank piece of paper. However, you may want to begin with these forms as you and your students explore literature circles together. The forms are included on the CD-ROM so that you can adapt them to meet your specific needs.

The *Literature Circles Resource Guide* includes both print and electronic components.

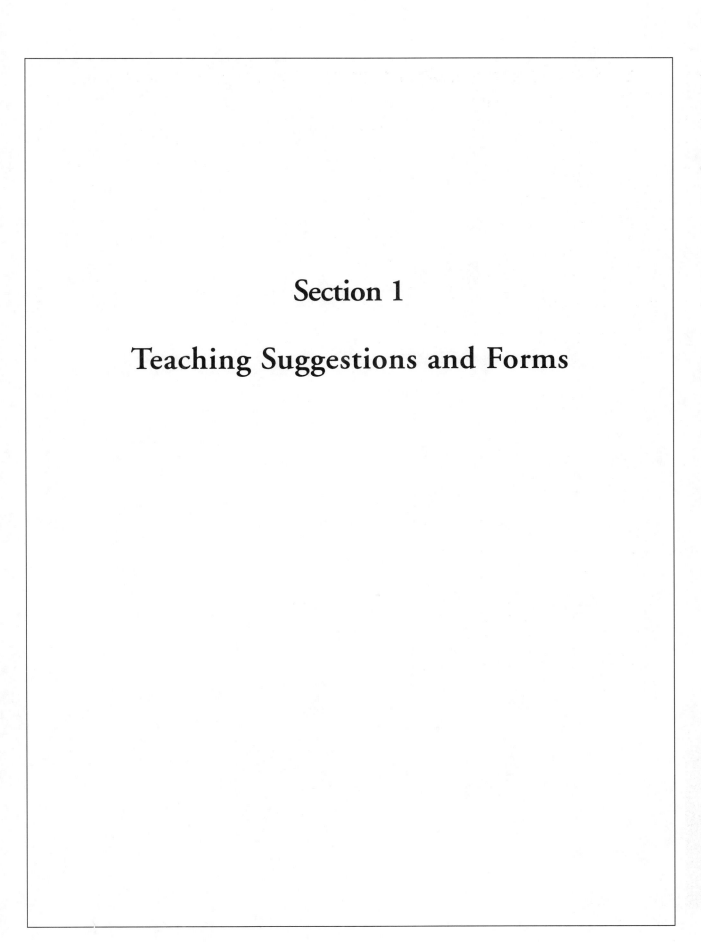

Section 1

Teaching Suggestions and Forms

Part 1

Literature Circles Organization

Regardless of the grade level you teach, literature circles share many common elements and require many teaching decisions. We begin by examining how literature circles may change over time. We provide examples of how two teachers envision literature circles throughout the year. In *Getting Started with Literature Circles* and *Literature Circles and Response*, we explain how literature circle units can be organized around fiction. Here we include two examples of how literature circles can also be developed around nonfiction texts and poetry. This section also contains forms to help students choose books and keep track of their reading. In addition, we provide forms to keep track of focus lessons on literature circle procedures and literacy skills and strategies. We conclude with end-of-unit and end-of-year debriefing forms to elicit student reflection on their participation and learning.

Teaching Suggestions

- *How Literature Circles Change Over Time* (p. 4)—Overview of the components of literature circles and how they evolve over time as teachers and students gain experience.
- *Samples of Teachers' Yearly Plans for Literature Circles* (pp. 6–7)—Chart showing two teachers' yearly plans for literature circles. Many teachers begin with only two or three literature circles per year and add more over time.
- *Literature Circles with Poetry and Nonfiction* (pp. 8–13)—Sample poetry unit for primary grade literature circles and a nonfiction unit for middle school students.

Forms for Organizing Literature Circles

- *Literature Circle Ballot* (p. 14)—Ballot for students to record their first, second, and third choices when literature circles are organized using book sets.
- *Literature Circle Bookmark* (pp. 15)—Bookmark on which students record the number of pages to be read (with room on the back to note questions and vocabulary words for discussion). Other examples of bookmarks can be found in the Discussion section.
- *Focus Lesson Checklists* (pp. 16–21)—Checklists to record specific focus lessons about literature circle procedures, reading strategies, writing and response strategies, and literature qualities (story structure, memorable language, literary elements, and genre characteristics). The forms include common focus lessons with space to add other strategies as the need arises. We also include a generic form for recording focus lessons.

Forms for Assessing and Evaluating Literature Circles Participation

- *Checklists and Self-Reflection* (pp. 22–24)— Forms to help students evaluate their participation in literature circles.
- *Book Club Rubric* (p. 25)—Example of a rubric based on class-developed criteria for literature circles participation. You can develop a rubric similar to this with your students

Literture Circles Organization

Literature Circles: Change Over Time

Component	Some First Steps	Some Next Steps	Some Later Steps
Teacher Beliefs	• There is only one "right" way to do literature circles	• There are many options for literature circles • I'll try out some, refine them, try others	• This is what works in my classroom • My students and I are constantly learning and changing how we do things
Goals	• Learning the structure and surviving • Choosing one component to focus on	• Refining structure • Learning how to discuss • Deepening meaning and engagement	• Developing meaningful response, higher levels of thinking • Using themes, nonfiction, poetry
Timeline: K – 1	• 1–2 weeks; no response project • 1–2 literature circle cycles, then other literacy activities	• ~ 1–2 weeks, including simple response project	• ~ 1–3 weeks with more elaborate response projects
2 – 8	• ~ 3–6 weeks • Emphasis on learning the process	• ~ 3–6 weeks • Emphasis on developing response	• ~ 3–6 weeks • Emphasis on deepening response
Schedule: K – 1	• Teacher sets schedule • Groups discuss once a week	• Teacher sets schedule or with student participation • Groups may discuss more than once a week	• Teacher sets schedule or with student participation • Groups may discuss more than once a week
2 – 8	• Teacher sets schedule • Groups discuss once a week	• Teacher and students set schedule together • Groups may discuss more often	• Groups decide how long entire book + extension will take and set own schedule
Choosing Books	• Whole class reads same book • Books chosen by teacher • Read from anthology/basal or whatever is available	• Two or three book choices • Books selected because they are engaging and meaningful	• Four or five book choices • Books selected because they relate to a theme, topic, genre, author, *and* represent good literature
Forming Groups	• Teacher gives book talks • Groups formed by student choice	• Teacher or students give book talks • Groups formed by student choice	• Teacher or students give book talks • Groups formed by student choice

Component	Some First Steps	Some Next Steps	Some Later Steps
Preparing for Discussion	• Teacher assigns response prompts • Students read alone, in pairs, with audio taped book, or with support	• Teacher offers choice of a few response prompts • Students/teacher generate responses	• Students choose from a menu of ideas or develop their own
Discussion	• Teacher sets discussion schedule • Teacher facilitates group; or teacher participates as group member; or teacher sits near group and observes; or students facilitate own groups, teacher roams • Use roles and forms	• Groups meet on a rotating basis • Students generate discussion guidelines • Modify/adapt forms	• Groups set their own schedule • Adapt forms or give them up entirely
Written Response	• Teacher assigns response prompts • Required response to each chapter/book • Try out a few forms	• Teacher offers choice of responses • Given number of responses required per week; written only • Modify/adapt forms	• Students choose from menu of ideas or develop their own • Flexible number of responses per week in variety of forms (e.g., written and art) • Modify or dispense with forms
Focus Lessons	• How to do literature circles • Literacy strategies, literary elements • Anything the teacher notices	• Refining literature circles • Literacy strategies, literary elements • Anything teacher/students notice	• Perfecting literature circles • Literacy strategies, literary elements • Anything teacher/students notice
Extension Projects	• Teacher assigns one option • Teacher decides: group or individual	• Teacher offers choice of options • Students decide: group or individual	• Students select from menu of options or develop their own • Students decide: group or individual
Assessment	• What assessment?	• Use one or two forms • Try out limited student self-assessment • Students choose a few responses to be graded; begin to evaluate discussion	• Modify forms and develop own instruments • Take and use anecdotal notes • Extensive student self-assessment • Students choose a few responses to be graded

Literature Circles Resource Guide

Yearly Literature Plan: Second Grade

September	Author Study: Patricia Polacco
October	Personal Challenges
November/December	Reaching Out to Others
January	Poetry
February/March	Freedom Fighters
April	Magical Journeys
May/June	Famous Artists

Overview of a One-Year Plan: Sixth Grade

Month	Books Topic/Theme/Genre	Teaching/Learning Focus
September – October	Whole class: *Roll of Thunder, Hear My Cry*	Learning process of literature circles Memorable language
November – January	Five books on homelessness (see Sample Book List)	Refining literature circles Understanding theme Fact vs. opinion Stereotypes
February	Egypt Genre Focus: Nonfiction	Refining literature circles Reading non-fiction Text elements: charts, graphs, glossary
March	Whole class: *Good Night, Mr. Tom*	Refining literature circles Vocabulary Using context clues
April	Five books on the Japanese-American internment during WWII (see Sample Book List)	Refining literature circles Understanding theme Point of view Author's craft
May	Five books by Walter Dean Myers (see Sample Book List)	Refining literature circles Author study Voice

Literture Circles Organization

Literature Circles with Poetry

Rationale

- invites natural discussions that lead children to add depth to their own poems they write in writing workshop
- gives the students an opportunity to discuss and evaluate a variety of poems
- promotes a love for poetry
- exposes children to a variety of poems
- encourages extensive rereading of poems
- provides time, choice, and peer/teacher response

Immersion

Immersing the children in poetry before you launch into literature circles is critical. The students receive their Poetry Pocket on the first day of school and we begin a year-long journey of reading and enjoying poetry. The Poetry Pocket is a folder to which we add one new poem each week. I photocopy the poem for the students and also copy the poem on a large wall chart. When I introduce a new poem, we first read it together as a whole group, then do a variety of choral readings. As the children become familiar with all the possibilities for choral reading, they begin to suggest how we choral read the new poem. This process takes about thirty to forty minutes each week.

Time Frame

Each session begins with a focus lesson that lasts approximately ten minutes. For our focus lessons we work on reading strategies: brainstorming criteria for quality poems, adding depth to oral discussions, fluent oral reading with expression, etc. Following the focus lessons, the students read poetry for about twenty-five minutes each day. As they read poems from their Poetry Pockets, they use "Post-it" notes to write comments about the poems they are reading. The children meet with their literature circle two days a week to discuss the poems. Following each meeting, the children debrief with their small literature circles and as a whole group. It is important to note that we begin a focus of poetry writing in writing workshop two weeks after we start literature circles with poetry. I invite the children to write five or more poems of their choice and publish these poems in a book.

Weeks 1 and 2

There are four students in each literature circle. On Monday and Wednesday during our reading time each student chooses one poem from their Poetry Pocket to discuss with the group. The children meet Tuesday and Thursday to discuss the poems. All the children bring their Poetry Pockets to the discussions each week. The children take turns sharing the poems they have chosen for the literature circle meeting. The student who chose the poem decides if he/she wants to read the poem to the group or if the group will read the poem chorally. I encourage the children to read each poem at least two times before they begin their discussion. The students share their personal reactions to the author's writing and evaluate the poems during their discussions. Their conversations last approximately twenty-five minutes. Following each literature circle meeting, the children reflect on the quality of their discussion and set goals for future literature circle meetings. As a whole group, we talk about the quality of the discussions and share effective discussion strategies.

Weeks 3 and 4

The children spend about thirty minutes reading poetry on Monday. I have two large tubs of poetry books in my room that the students can choose from. They also bring poetry books from home and check some books out at the library. While they are reading on Monday, their job is to find one new poem they want to share with their literature circle the next day. Once the children find their poem, they place a "Post-it" note on the page and write their name on the sticky note. I make four copies of each poem, one for each member of the literature circle.

On Tuesday, I give the children the four new poems their literature circle members have selected for them to read and discuss. The children spend the first twenty to thirty minutes reading the four new poems. They read the poems several times independently or with a partner. Immediately following the reading of the poems, the students meet with their literature circle to begin their conversations. Once again, the children respond aesthetically to each poem and discuss what makes the poems quality poetry. After the children reflect on their discussion with their literature circle, we debrief as a whole class, sharing what made their discussions effective, as well as possible changes for the future. The children add the four new poems to their Poetry Pockets.

On Wednesday, the children follow the same routine they did on Monday. Each child spends time reading and chooses one new poem to share with his/her literature circle. The students' routine on Thursday is identical to the routine on Tuesday. The students read the four new poems and discuss them with their literature circle. Once again, the children debrief as a small group, then with the entire class.

Week 5

For week five, we follow the same routine as weeks 3 and 4. The only change is by this time the children are beginning to publish some of their own poems in writing workshop. The children are given the option of choosing one of their own poems to share and discuss with their literature circle on Tuesday or Thursday.

The Nile Diner

The main goal of this nonfiction literature circle unit is to help students recognize and develop reading strategies for nonfiction text. Many of these strategies develop naturally while students are reading nonfiction material, while others need to be taught.

On the very first day of the unit, the students brainstorm all the ways they read nonfiction material differently than fiction. I list these ideas on poster paper and keep the list hanging in the classroom during the whole unit. The students and I add to the list as new strategies are discovered or taught.

After the brainstorming I hand out the Nile Diner Menu. The purpose of the menu is to lay out the unit plan clearly to the students and to encourage self-management. Students have four weeks to complete all sections of the menu. During the fifth week we celebrate their accomplishments through presentations of the "desserts."

The "appetizers" are books about Egypt that really need to be read cover to cover, more like a novel. Many of them are written in story form and are historical fiction or folk tales, but contain many facts about Ancient Egypt. It is in this section that students discover the importance of reading epilogues and author's notes to distinguish fact from fiction.

The "main course" books are more typical, fact laden nonfiction books. While reading these books, students discover they don't have to read all books cover to cover to learn new information. Of all the nonfiction reading strategies learned during this unit, this one seems to be the most liberating. Many children are overwhelmed with the thought of reading a whole book filled with facts. Another sigh of relief can be heard throughout the room when students realize that it is all right to skip around the book and read the pages in any order they want. During the reading of the books in this category, we also focus on the importance of glossaries, the table of contents, captions under pictures, and the pictures themselves as tools for finding and learning new information.

Students are required to read one book from the "appetizer" list and three from the "main course" list. Throughout the unit, all the books are displayed on the chalk trays and tables in the classroom. Within these guidelines, students choose which books to read and in what order. During the course of the four weeks, students meet in literature circle groups to discuss three of the four books they have read. I determine the groups and schedule one discussion each week, notifying the students well in advance what day their group will be meeting so they have the opportunity to get prepared. When the discussions occur, usually each student is talking about a different book since there are so many to choose from. Before the first discussion, we talk about how it will differ from our usual literature circles. I take this opportunity to caution students about the discussion turning into "show and tell." We brainstorm ways to avoid this and talk about the value of an interactive discussion versus everyone sitting and listening while one student at a time talks about his or her book. Students come to value comparing and contrasting facts and the building of understanding about the topic that takes place during a discussion. They realize this doesn't happen by taking turns to talk about each book.

Students are also required to write a book review after reading each of the four books they choose. This component of the unit, called "paying the bill," gives me additional material for assessment and helps students focus on what they learned from each book. It also prepares them for their discussion. Because I ask them to identify which nonfiction reading strategies they used while reading the book, it helps them to think about themselves as readers and what new strategies they are developing. The directions are clearly outlined on the Nile Diner Menu and I provide high quality samples from previous years so that students have a clear idea of my expectations. These four reviews are placed in a folder with some representation of Ancient Egyptian culture on the cover. This may be done in whatever medium the student chooses.

Throughout the course of the unit, students are also thinking about and planning which "dessert" they will choose and who they will work with. I always give the option of working individually or in groups from their discussion group. I also require that students not begin work on their project until they have finished reading the four books they have chosen and have written a review for each book.

During the fifth and final week of the unit, students present their "desserts." An emphasis is placed not only on the quality of their project, but also on the quality of the presentation. The goal is to share new information learned about Ancient Egypt with the rest of the class. This is always a fun and rewarding experience filled with creative expression. It also gives me another opportunity for assessment. The "bill" is collected during this final week of the unit.

Literature Circles with Nonfiction

The Nile Diner Menu
Appetizers (Choose One)

Tales Mummies Tell by Patricia Lauber

Egyptian Pyramid by Elizabeth Longley

Tutankhamen's Gift by Robert Sabuda

The Egyptian Cinderella by Shirley Climo

Cleopatra by Diane Stanley and Peter Vennema

The Egyptian Echo by Paul Dowswell

Nefertari: Princess of Egypt by Roberta Angeletti

The Gods and Goddesses of Ancient Egypt by Leonard Everett Fisher

The Winged Cat: A Tale of Ancient Egypt by Deborah Nourse Lattimore

The Pharaohs of Ancient Egypt by Elizabeth Payne

Main Course (Choose Three)

First Facts About Ancient Egyptians by Jacqueline Morley

An Egyptian Pyramid by Jacqueline Morley

Ancient Egypt by George Hart

How Would You Survive as an Ancient Egyptian? by Jacqueline Morley and David Salariya

Egyptian Town by Scott Steedman

Science in Ancient Egypt by Geraldine Woods

Who Built the Pyramids? by Jane Chisholm and Struan Reid

Pharaohs and Pyramids by Tony Alan

The Best Book of Mummies by Philip Steele

Ancient Egypt by Judith Crosher

Ancient Egyptians by Fiona MacDonald

Secrets of the Mummies by Shelley Tanaka

Tutankhamun: The Life and Death of a Pharaoh by David Murdoch

Pyramids by Anne Millard

Cultural Atlas for Young People: Ancient Egypt by Geraldine Harris

The Egyptians: History, Society, Religion by Renzo Tossi

The Pharaohs of Ancient Egypt by Claire Derouin

The Awesome Egyptians by Terry Deary and Peter Hepplewhite

Dessert (Choose One)

"The Egyptian Tour"

Acting as a tour guide, take us on a trip through Egypt, making stops at important places along the way. Present your itinerary to the class, including details about the attractions. You will need to create visual aids and become knowledgeable about the many unusual sights of this country as you prepare your presentation.

"The Actor's Delight"

Present a skit that portrays life in Egypt or focuses on the life of a well-known person, such as Cleopatra or King Tutankhamun.

"The Pyramid"

Construct a pyramid from tagboard. Illustrate the outside of each of the four sections with a drawing of something about Egypt that you find interesting. On the inside of each of the four sections, write an explanation of the corresponding illustration.

"Illustrated Timeline"

Create a timeline with events and key people from Egypt. Include illustrations to highlight special events and historical figures.

"Fact Finder"

Explore one topic you found particularly interesting while reading about Egypt. Write a research report, delving into details about this topic. Share your information with the class in a presentation that includes visual aids such as slides, an overhead projector, or a computer.

Paying the Bill

Place the four Book Reviews you have written into a folder that you have designed to reflect some aspect of Ancient Egyptian culture. Be sure to bind the folder in some way to hold the contents inside. Decorate the folder to reflect some aspect of Egyptian culture.

Literature Circle Ballot

Name: _____   Date: _____

1. _____

2. _____

3. _____

Literature Circle Ballot

Name: _____   Date: _____

1. _____

2. _____

3. _____

Literature Circle Ballot

Name: _____   Date: _____

1. _____

2. _____

3. _____

Literature Circle Bookmark

Please record the number of pages your literature circle group decides to read each day.

Monday _____

Tuesday _____

Wednesday _____

Thursday _____

Friday _____

You may use the back of your bookmark to write **questions** you want to ask or **vocabulary words** you may want to discuss.

Literature Circle Bookmark

Please record the number of pages your literature circle group decides to read each day.

Monday _____

Tuesday _____

Wednesday _____

Thursday _____

Friday _____

You may use the back of your bookmark to write **questions** you want to ask or **vocabulary words** you may want to discuss.

15

Literature Circle Bookmark

Please record the number of pages your literature circle group decides to read each day.

Monday _____

Tuesday _____

Wednesday _____

Thursday _____

Friday _____

You may use the back of your bookmark to write **questions** you want to ask or **vocabulary words** you may want to discuss.

Literature Circles Resource Guide

Literture Circles Organization

Focus Lesson Checklist: Literature Circles Procedures

Focus Lesson:	Dates Taught		
How to choose a book			
How to start the discussion quickly			
How to listen attentively			
How to keep the conversation going			
The role of a discussion group member			
What to write in your response journal			
What to do when you don't understand part of the book			
What to do when your group finishes			
How to mediate conflicts			
How to spice up a lagging discussion			
How to tie extension projects back to the book			

Focus Lesson Checklist: Reading Strategies

Focus Lesson:	Dates Taught		
Using what you already know (background knowledge)			
Previewing			
Predicting			
Reading on to see if predictions make sense			
Identifying important information			
Thinking about what would make sense			
Self-correcting when reading doesn't make sense			
Creating pictures in your head			
Using flexible strategies to identify unknown words			
Reading what you don't know slowly and what you do know quickly			
Asking yourself (or the text) questions			
Finding evidence to support a point			
Comparing/contrasting			
Building vocabulary through reading			
Analyzing, interpreting, inferring			

Literature Circles Organization

Focus Lesson Checklist: Writing and Response Strategies

Focus Lesson:	Dates Taught		
Choosing a topic or focus for your journal entry			
Supporting ideas with information from the book, your own life, or other books			
Elaborating by using details			
Writing with a purpose and for an audience			
Trying out dialogue			
Using figurative and descriptive language			
Using sketches and illustrations to spark or extend ideas			
Developing criteria for effective writing			
Writing a response from a character's point of view			
Incorporating ideas from "Post-it" notes into a written response			
Incorporating ideas raised during discussion into a written response			

Focus Lesson Checklist: Literature Qualities

Focus Lesson: Story Structure	Dates Taught		
Beginnings			
Climax			
Endings			
Problems or attempts to solve problem			
Beginning, middle, end			
Focus Lesson: Memorable Language	Dates Taught		
Interesting words and phrases			
Action verbs			
Descriptive details			
Alliteration			
Similes, metaphors, analogy			
Synonyms			

Focus Lesson Checklist: Literature Qualities (cont.)

Focus Lesson: Literary Elements	Dates Taught		
Character			
Plot			
Setting			
Theme			
Point of view and perspective			
Tone and mood			
Persuasive devices			

Focus Lesson: Genre Characteristics	Dates Taught		
Realistic fiction			
Historical fiction			
Fantasy and science fiction			
Traditional literature (folktale, myth, legend, tale)			
Poetry			
Biography and autobiography			
Informational books			

Focus Lessons

Date	T/S	Focus Lesson

Literature Circles Organization

Key: T=Teacher-Led   S=Student-Led

Classroom Based Assessment   Copyright © 2001 Christopher-Gordon Publishers

Literture Circles Organization

Literature Circles Checklist

Name: _____   **Date:** _____

Title: _____   **Author:** _____

Evaluate yourself each day on your participation during literature circles.

☺ I did my best.

😐 I did O.K.

☹ Not this time.

Date	Finished Reading	Date	Finished Writing	Date	Participated in Discussion	Listened to Others

Comments:

Literature Circles Reflection

Name: _____   **Date:** _____

1. Did you enjoy Literature Circles this year? Why? _____

_____

_____

2. Which of the following did you like doing?

    ❑ Reading at home with your parents

    ❑ Talking about the book at school

    ❑ Writing in your journal

    ❑ Signing up on Friday

    ❑ Choosing your first/second choice

    ❑ Doing a project with the book

3. What were your favorite books?

_____

_____

_____

_____

4. What did you learn from Literature Circles?

_____

_____

_____

Literature Circles Self-Evaluation

Name: _____   **Date:** _____

5 = Always
4 = Almost all of the time   Title: _____
3 = Sometimes
2 = Occasionally   Author: _____
1 = Never

_____ I had my novel and response journal ready at the beginning of each meeting.

_____ I was quiet and listened for directions.

_____ I wrote thoughtfully in my response journal.

_____ I dated my journal entries.

_____ I remembered to write down important quotes, new or interesting words, and items to be discussed in the group (using "Post-it" notes, a bookmark, or journal).

_____ I stayed on task during reading and discussion sessions.

_____ I took an active role during discussions by *asking questions, listening,* and *talking* about the book.

_____ I was cooperative and participated in the extension activity.

What did you like most about this book? _____

_____

_____

What is your goal for the next book? What do you plan on doing differently during your next literature circle to make yourself a better reader/participator?

_____

_____

_____

Literature Extension Activity
(Complete after watching the video of your presentation.)

What went well? _____

_____

_____

What will you work on next time? _____

_____

Book Club Rubric

4	• I read all of the assigned reading. • I made a good effort on my written assignment. • I was eager to share and I contributed to the discussion to keep it going. • I used good listening skills all of the time.
3	• I read most of the assigned reading. • I did a minimal amount of assigned writing. • I participated a little in the discussion. • I used good listening skills most of the time.
2	• I read a little of the book. • I did not do the assigned writing. • I seldom participated in the discussion. • I used good listening skills sometimes. • I was not prepared to discuss.
1	• I did not read the book. • I was not prepared. • I did not participate in the discussion. • I did not use good listening skills. • I did not bring my materials.

Part 2

Oral Response: Discussions

Discussion is at the heart of literature circles. Talking about books helps readers construct meaning collaboratively. In the process, students strengthen their own understanding and become more actively involved with what they read. Effective discussion skills need to be taught, modeled, and practiced so that literature circle conversations become more than turn taking or rote recitation and evolve into true interactions among readers.

Several ideas described in the next section on Written Response (such as the Journal Prompts and Golden Lines) can also be used to prompt and support student discussions.

Teaching Suggestions

- *What Makes a Good Discussion?* (p. 29)—Sample list of components of an effective discussion. These guidelines were used to develop the "Good Discussion: Self-Reflection" form on page 21. You can develop a chart similar to this jointly with your students as you talk about and model discussion skills.
- *Tools for Discussion* (p. 30)—Ways to help students prepare for literature discussions.
- *Preparing for Discussions* (p. 31)—Simple guidelines to help students prepare for literature circle discussions.
- *Literature Circles Guidelines* (p. 32)—Chart of expectations for student participation before and during discussion. These guidelines were used to develop the student "Literature Circle Evaluation" form on page 16. You can develop a chart similar to this in consultation with your students.
- *Questions for Discussion* (p. 33)—A more extensive list of the types of things students can talk about during discussions.
- *Literature Circles Discussion Starters* (p. 34)—Comment card with prompts to aid students in learning the social graces of discussion.
- *Discussion Etiquette* (p. 35)—Sample chart of discussion etiquette. Introduce the discussion elements, then brainstorm with your students what each element "looks like" and "sounds like." (The shaded areas are to be completed with your students.)

Forms for Discussion

- *Bookmarks* (pp. 36–37)—Forms on which students record words, questions, and ideas to prompt discussion.
- *Literature Circles Discussion Log* (p. 38)—Form for quick notation of personal response, questions, and "wonder words." Students may want to write more in a response journal after the discussion.
- *Literature Response Log* (p. 39)—Includes room to record a short journal response, points for discussion, and a self-evaluation checklist.

Forms for Assessing and Evaluating Discussion

- *Evaluation and Self-Reflection* (pp. 40–45)—Evaluation forms for students to reflect upon their participation in and contribution to discussions. The "Good Discussion: Self-reflection" form on page 21 was developed based on the guidelines, "What Makes a Good Discussion" presented on page 4. Similarly, the "Literature Circles Evaluation" form on page 16 aligns with "Literature Circles Guidelines" on page 8. You may want to alter these forms to reflect the guidelines that you and your students develop.

- *Rubrics* (pp. 46–47)—We have included a generic rubric for discussion. You and your students can determine the criteria for each rating. We also provide a more extensive rubric that specifies the criteria for each rating.

- *Anecdotal Notes* (pp. 48–50)—Focus questions and anecdotal record-keeping forms to guide teacher assessment of discussions.

What Makes a Good Discussion?

- **Empathetic Listening:** Give your complete attention to the speakers, showing the people in your group that you value their thoughts.

  – Use positive body language
  – Eye contact
  – Hands resting

- **Responding to Group Members:** Expand on other group members' ideas by sharing your thoughts and feelings about what they contributed to the conversations.

- **Clarifying:** Probe to understand each other's ideas better.

  – Tell me more about . . .
  – What do you mean . . .?
  – Why do you think . . .?

- **Sharing Ideas and Justifying Opinions:** Share parts of the book that are important to you and explain why they are important. Justify your opinions.

  – I think . . . . because . . .
  – I wonder . . .
  – I was surprised . . .
  – This part reminds me of . . .
  – I don't understand . . .
  – I like this section of writing because . . .
  – I noticed . . .
  – I wish . . .
  – My favorite part is . . . . because . . .

- **Self-reflection:** Consider what has been done well, and make decisions about what needs to be improved. Set goals for the future.

Oral Response Discussions

Tools for Discussion

Brainstorming Ideas—With your students, brainstorm some ideas about what they can talk about during discussions.

Quote and Question—As students read, ask them to find one quote that stood out for them and raise one question that genuinely puzzled them.

Prompts—(See Journal Prompts, p. 52)

Guided Topic—You may want to suggest a topic for discussion that you introduce through a focus lesson. This is a good way to tie in a focus on theme, genre, or author.

Student-generated Questions—Generate a list of open-ended questions with your students.

"Post-it" Notes—These small "flags" work well to identify passages that students want to share in a discussion. As they read, students can make short notes or write questions on the "Post-it" notes to remind them of what they want to discuss.

Bookmarks—Students can use bookmarks to note interesting or puzzling words they encounter, to write questions, and to record ideas worth discussing.

Golden Lines—"Golden lines"—quotes from the book—are an easy and effective source of interesting discussion material. Many students find it much easier to select something the author said than to come up with their own reactions.

Discussion Log—Discussion logs are a more structured way to prompt students to collect quotes, questions, and interesting words. They provide just enough space for a quick notation and differ from a journal entry, whose purpose is extended and reflective response.

Preparing for Discussions

Before you meet with your literature circle, choose a part of your book that:

- makes you wonder
- makes you laugh
- makes you sad or upset
- you don't understand
- was your favorite part
- has interesting words
- reminds you of another book
- reminds you of something that has happened in your life

Mark the parts you want to discuss or make a note in your journal about them. Be ready to talk about your choices.

Oral Response Discussions

Literature Circles Guidelines

I am looking for:

1. Getting Started in One Minute

- quickly & quietly carry your chairs to your spot, open books, and begin reading or discussion

2. Reading and Following Along

- sit knee to knee
- look at book
- gently help others with words they don't know

3. Cooperation

- get along
- work out disagreements
- encourage members of your circle
- respect others' ideas and opinions

4. Discussion

- ask questions
- support ideas and opinions
- disagree politely
- listen: eyes and ears on speaker
- vary responses (e.g., I notice . . . , I think . . . , I feel . . . , I wonder . . . This reminds me of . . .)

Questions for Discussion

- Who is your favorite character? Why?

- Who do the characters remind you of?

- Why do you think a character did _____?
  What would you have done?

- If you could be friends with any characters in the book, which ones would you choose? Why?

- Could this story really have happened?

- Do these characters remind you of characters in other books? Which ones? Why?

- How does the book relate to your life?

- How did you feel when you read the book?

- Is there a scene you can picture in your mind? If so, what does it look like?

- How do you think the book will end?

- What "golden lines" caught your eye as a reader?

Oral Response Discussions

Literature Circles Discussion Starters

Excuse me . . .

I'd like to add . . .

I disagree . . .

I agree because . . .

I don't understand what you mean . . .

I'm confused about . . .

This comment card can be taped to the table where discussions take place, copied onto a poster displayed in the classroom, or taped into each student's literature circles journal.

Discussion Etiquette

Discussion Elements	Looks Like:	Sounds Like:

Focused on Discussion
    Body posture
    Eye contact
	Eyes on speaker
	Hands empty
	Sit up
	Mind is focused
	Face speaker
		Speaker's voice only
		Paying attention
		Appropriate responses
		Voices low
		One voice at a time

Active Participation
    Respond to ideas
    Share feelings
	Eyes on speaker
	Hands to yourself
	Hands empty
	Talking one at a time
	Head nodding
		Appropriate responses
		Follow off others' ideas
		Nice comments
		Positive attitudes

Asking Questions for Clarification	Listening Hands empty	Positive, nice questions Polite answers
Piggybacking Off Others' Ideas	Listening Paying attention	Positive, nice talking Wait for people to finish
Disagreeing Constructively	Look at the speaker Nice face, nice looks	Polite responses Let people finish talking Quiet voices No put downs
Active Listening	Paying attention Hands empty Looking at the speaker	Quiet Speaker's voice only
Taking Turns to Let Others Speak	One person talking Attention on the speaker	One voice
Supporting Opinions with Evidence	Use the book and form	Piggybacking off others Help others find evidence One voice Let people finish talking
Encouraging Others	Eyes on speaker Head nodding	Positive responses Appropriate responses

Oral Response Discussions

Oral Response Discussions

Bookmark

• WORDS:

• QUESTIONS?

Bookmark

• WORDS:

• QUESTIONS?

Bookmark

• WORDS:

• QUESTIONS?

Getting Started with Literature Circles

Bookmark

Name: _____

Title: _____

Author: _____

List favorite or important pages, quotes, scenes, interesting or unknown words.

_____

_____

_____

_____

_____

_____

_____

_____

_____

_____

_____

_____

_____

_____

_____

_____

_____

Bookmark

Name: _____

Title: _____

Author: _____

List favorite or important pages, quotes, scenes, interesting or unknown words.

_____

_____

_____

_____

_____

_____

_____

_____

_____

_____

_____

_____

_____

_____

_____

_____

_____

Oral Response Discussions

Literature Circles Discussion Log

Name: _____

Title and Author: _____

For Discussion Date: _____   Reading Assignment: _____

A part that I would like to share with my group: (Write the first and last word and the page number.)

_____

One question that I have about the reading: _____

_____

Wonder Words: Write three words from your reading that you wonder about and want to talk about with your group.

_____   _____   _____

- -

Literature Circles Discussion Log

Name: _____

Title and Author: _____

For Discussion Date: _____   Reading Assignment: _____

A part that I would like to share with my group: (Write the first and last word and the page number.)

_____

One question that I have about the reading: _____

_____

Wonder Words: Write three words from your reading that you wonder about and want to talk about with your group.

_____   _____   _____

Literature Response Log

Name: _____   Pages: ____ Date: _____

Title: _____   Author: _____

Response

_____

_____

_____

_____

_____

_____

Points for Discussion

I'd like to talk to my group about . . . I'd like to ask them . . . I wonder why . . . It was interesting that/when . . .

_____

_____

_____

_____

Are You Ready?

❑ I finished my assigned reading
❑ I dated and labeled my responses
❑ I put my best effort into my work

❑ I completed my responses
❑ I marked the parts I wanted to share

Getting Started with Literature Circles

Oral Response Discussions

Literature Circles Evaluation

Name: _____ **Date:** _____

Literature Circle Group: _____

Book: _____

What things did your group do very well today?

☐ started in 1 minute

☐ read and followed along

☐ cooperated

☐ discussed well

What things are going really well in your discussions?

☐ listening to others

☐ everyone is sharing

☐ predicting what will happen next

☐ asking questions

☐ supporting ideas

☐ relating to other books or characters

☐ relating to own lives

Discussion Evaluation

Name: _____ Date: _____

What things am I doing well in my literature circle?

_____

_____

_____

_____

_____

What things could I do to help my literature circle go better?

_____

_____

_____

_____

_____

Oral Response Discussions

Literature Discussion Self-Evaluation

Name: _____ **Date:** _____

Title: _____ **Author:** _____

What did I do well during our literature discussion? (asked good questions, listened actively, responded to others, supported my ideas using the book, took a risk, compared the book to my life or other books) Give specific examples.

_____

_____

_____

_____

_____

_____

_____

_____

What could I do better next time?

_____

_____

_____

_____

_____

_____

_____

_____

Discussion Summary/Group Feedback

Name: _____   **Date:** _____

Title: _____   **Author:** _____

Summarize what you did well and/or learned today during your literature discussion.

_____

_____

_____

_____

_____

Comments from other group members:

1. _____

_____

_____

2. _____

_____

_____

3. _____

_____

_____

4. _____

_____

_____

Oral Response Discussions

Literature Circles Debriefing

Name: _____   Date: _____

Title: _____   Author: _____

How much did you participate in the discussion about this book?

☐ about the right amount   ☐ too much   ☐ not at all   ☐ too little

_____

_____

What was an important contribution you made to the discussion?

_____

_____

What was an important idea or explanation expressed by someone else in the group during the discussions? (Identify the person and tell what he/she said.)

_____

_____

What group strategies did your group use well? (participating, staying on topic, contributing appropriate information, encouraging others to contribute, listening carefully, making good eye contact, being considerate of others' opinions, asking for clarification, summarizing, using appropriate voice levels)

_____

_____

_____

What strategies did you struggle with?

_____

_____

_____

Suggestions/comments/goals for next literature circle discussion:

_____

_____

Oral Response Discussions

Discussion: Self-Reflection

Name: _____   **Date:** _____

Title: _____   **Author:** _____

	Yes	Sometimes	Not Yet
I was an empathetic listener by giving my complete attention.	☐	☐	☐
I responded to other group members' ideas.	☐	☐	☐
I asked questions to clarify my understanding of the book and/or to help me better understand other group members' ideas.	☐	☐	☐
I shared parts of the book that were important to me and explained why they were important.	☐	☐	☐

What is a new insight or appreciation you gained today during your discussion? (*Did you learn something new about the book? What do you remember most about the discussion?*)

_____

_____

_____

_____

Goal: Next time, I want to work on _____

_____

_____

_____

_____

Oral Response Discussions

Rubric

4 WOW! TERRIFIC!	
3 You've Got It!	
2 Not Yet	
1 Try Again!	

Discussion Rubric

Name: _____   **Date:** _____

Check the boxes that apply to this discussion, then mark an "X" in the top bar to indicate approximate placement on a continuum. Use the back for comments: what you noticed as strengths and weaknesses, and what you found interesting and unique.

NOVICE	APPRENTICE	PRACTITIONER	EXPERT
☐ not prepared for discussion (forgets journal or book)	☐ brings book and journal	☐ brings book with passages marked and several journal entries	☐ brings book with passages clearly marked and thoughtful journal entries
☐ rarely contributes to discussion	☐ contributes to discussions occasionally or when prompted	☐ contributes appropriately to discussions	☐ contributes significantly to discussion
☐ conversation off-task or does not contribute	☐ difficulty keeping discussion going	☐ generally keeps the discussion going	☐ effectively keeps the discussion going
☐ rarely listens or responds to group members	☐ sometimes listens and responds appropriately, occasionally asks questions or shares ideas	☐ listens and responds adequately (occasionally reads journal entries or unclear passages, discusses unknown words, asks questions, listens actively, builds on others' comments, makes connections to other books and experiences, discusses author's style and literary elements)	☐ listens and responds thoughtfully (reads journal entries or unclear passages, discusses unknown words, asks questions, listens actively, builds on others' comments, makes connections to other books and experiences, discusses author's style and literary elements)

Comments:

Classroom Based Assessment

Copyright © 2001 Christopher-Gordon Publishers

Oral Response Discussions

Focus Questions for Anecdotal Notes: Literature Discussions

1. Is the student prepared for the literature discussion?

2. Does the student use the text to share passages? To support ideas and opinions? How effectively?

3. Does the student listen actively to others?

4. Does the student ask questions? What kinds?

5. Do the questions get a thoughtful response? Which are most effective?

6. Does the student contribute thoughtful ideas?

7. Does the student make predictions? How effectively?

8. Does the student build on other people's comments?

9. Does the student keep the group on task?

10. Does the student discuss unknown or interesting words?

11. Does the student make personal connections to his/her life? At what levels?

12. Does the student make connections to other books, authors, and experiences?

13. Does the student discuss the author's craft and word choice?

14. Does the student discuss literary elements (plot, setting, characters)?

15. Can the student reflect on literature circle participation and set goals?

Anecdotal Records for:

Oral Response Discussions

Classroom Based Assessment

Literature Discussion Notes

Book Title: _____   **Date:** _____

Record student responses which indicate any of the following: showing enjoyment, sharing reactions, seeking meaning from illustrations, drawing conclusions, elaborating, justifying, explaining, expressing feelings, relating to personal experiences, going beyond "I like" statements, making predictions, asking questions, discussing literary elements.

Oral Response Discussions

Part 3

Written Response: Journals

Response journals are thinking tools. Engagement occurs when readers slow down long enough to respond to the text. When used during literature circles, response journals can help readers remember what they have read. They also offer a place to raise questions and comment on characters, events, and issues.

Teaching Suggestions

- *Journal Prompts* (p. 52)—Simple response starters to prompt students to write about what they are reading. These prompts can also provide support for literature circle discussions.
- *Journal Response Forms* (p. 53)—A variety of forms to guide written response.

Forms for Written Response

- *Golden Lines* (p. 54)—Form on which students can collect significant quotes from their reading. Students can share their Golden Lines during discussions or incorporate the quotes into their written responses and/or extension projects.

Forms for Assessing and Evaluating Written Response

- *Rubrics* (pp.55–57)—Evaluation rubrics used by students and teachers for individual entries and for the entire journal.
- *Journal Comments* (p. 58)—Form for teachers to evaluate and comment on students' completed response journal.
- *Assessing Response to Literature: Primary and Intermediate* (pp. 59–60)—Checklists for primary and intermediate grade teachers to assess the developmental progression of written responses to literature.

Journal Prompts

- I liked _____ because . . .

- I noticed . . .

- I wonder . . .

- I felt _____ because . . .

- I think . . .

- This story makes me think of . . .

- I wish . . .

- If I were _____, I would . . .

- When I . . .

- I was surprised by . . .

Journal Response Forms

Diary Entries—Choose an incident or event from your story that might cause one of the characters to respond in a journal. Taking the role of the character, explain what happened and how you felt about it. You might want to create journal entries for more than one day in your character's life.

Cause/Effect Explanation—Find a place in your book where something happened as a result of an action taken by a character or by an event that occurred. On one side of your paper, illustrate what you see as the cause. Write a brief explanation underneath. On the other side, illustrate the result and write your explanation.

Letters—Write a letter to a friend, to your literature circle group, to a character in your book, or to the author. Share your thoughts, questions, and feelings about the book so far.

Character Web—Draw a portrait of your selected character in the middle of your journal page. List three to five traits that describe that character; write these around the character's portrait. (Adaptation: Now find a specific passage from your book to support each trait. Copy that passage next to the trait. Be sure to list the page number.)

Sketching and Drawing—Use shape, design, image, and color to represent what you feel about your book. You might want to recreate a significant scene, depict how a character is feeling, capture the mood or tone of the events in this chapter, illustrate the conflict, or portray your feelings about this book at this point in your reading.

Copyright © 2001 Christopher-Gordon Publishers

Written Response: Journals

Golden Lines

_____

_____

_____

_____

_____

_____

_____

_____

_____

_____

_____

_____

_____

_____

Response Journal Rubric

Name: _____   Date: _____

Title: _____   Author: _____

4   In addition to a precise plot summary, the writer makes inferences, predictions, comparisons, or evaluations and supports ideas with evidence from the story. The writer makes connections with his/her life, other books, or other events. The writer demonstrates fluency.

3   The plot is accurately summarized with specific details. The writer shares one or more personal reflections and gives examples to support his/her interpretations.

2   The plot is summarized in a general way but lacks detail or support. The writer may share a general personal response.

1   The writer retells minimal details from the story.

Written Response: Journals

Rubric for Literature Circle Journals

4	• Includes at least four suggestions from the class-generated list of Quality Journal Entries • Illustrations are complete and add meaning and interest • Work is neat • Ideas are well developed • Conventions are correct
3	• Includes at least two suggestions from our list • Illustrations are incomplete • Ideas are not well developed
2	• Very little writing • Work is sloppy • No illustrations • Writing does not relate to the book
1	• No journal

Comments:

Journal Response Rubric

Name: _____   **Date:** _____

Check the boxes that apply to this journal response, then mark an "X" in the top bar to indicate approximate placement on a continuum. Use the back for comments: what you noticed as strengths and weaknesses, and what you found interesting and unique.

NOVICE	APPRENTICE	PRACTITIONER	EXPERT
☐ little writing	☐ some writing (includes reactions, summaries, and connections to other books or experiences, evaluates and analyzes)	☐ adequate writing (includes occasional reactions, summaries, and connections to other books or experiences, evaluates and analyzes author's craft or elements of literature)	☐ thorough writing (includes thoughtful reactions, summaries, and connections to other books or experiences, evaluates and analyzes author's craft or elements of literature)
☐ includes no examples to support opinions	☐ includes occasional, incomplete or unclear examples to support opinions	☐ includes sufficient examples to support opinions	☐ includes clear, complete examples to support opinions
☐ no variation in forms of written response	☐ occasionally varies forms of written response	☐ clearly varies forms of written response	☐ skillfully and creatively varies forms of written response
☐ no attention to details (lacking in organization and neatness with many spelling and punctuation errors)	☐ slight attention to details (lacking in organization and neatness with some spelling and punctuation errors)	☐ adequate attention to details (somewhat organized and neat, with mostly correct spelling and punctuation)	☐ thorough attention to details (well organized and neat, with correct spelling and punctuation)

Comments:

Classroom Based Assessment

Written Response: Journals

Journal Comments

Name: _____   **Date:** _____

Title: _____   **Author:** _____

Cover
(title, author, student name, illustration, page numbers, neat appearance)

_____

_____

_____

_____

Written Response: Journals

Journal Entries
(dated, varied format, comments supported with examples/details, neat appearance)

_____

_____

_____

_____

Vocabulary
(*at least* 10 words and definitions to talk about)

_____

_____

Total Score Based on Journal Response Rubric _____

_____

_____

Assessing Response to Literature: Primary

Name:

Date / Title	Literal Level	Personal Reaction	Prediction	Summarizes Retells	Supports Justifies	Other Points of View	Evaluates	Discusses Author's Craft	Comments

59

Written Response: Journals

Written Response: Journals

Assessing Response to Literature: Intermediate

Name:

Date / Title	Personal Reaction	Prediction	Summarizes Retells	Supports Justifies	Other Points of View	Evaluates Analyzes	Discusses Author's Craft/Theme	Discusses Literary Elements	Connects to Other Books and Authors	Comments

Part 4

Extension Projects

The purpose of an extension project is just what the name implies—to *extend* the reading experience by responding to the entire book. In addition to talking and writing, responding through art, music, and drama deepens students' understanding. When readers culminate a literature circle unit with an extension project, they may revisit what they have read, continue the conversations (and the discoveries), and reach for deeper understanding.

For more information about the extension projects mentioned in these forms, refer to chapter 10 in *Literature Circles and Response* and chapter 8 in *Getting Started with Literature Circles*.

Teaching Suggestions

- *Literature Extension Projects* (p. 62)—Samples of beginning projects, as well as more complex and more time-consuming project ideas.
- *Extension Project Focus Questions* (p. 63)—Questions to guide students as they plan and evaluate their extension projects.
- *Book Projects and Genres, Letter, and Rubric* (pp. 64–66)—One teacher's ideas for matching extension projects with specific genres. We include an example of a letter she sends home explaining the assignment and the matching evaluation rubric.

Forms for Planning Extension Projects

- *Extension Planning* (pp. 67–70)—Forms for students to use as they plan their extension projects and demonstrate how their projects extend their understanding of the book.

Forms for Assessing and Evaluating Extension Projects and Presentations

- *Response Project Evaluations, Self-Reflection, and Rubrics* (pp. 71–77)—Forms and rubrics to guide student self-reflection and evaluation of extension projects and process.
- *Presentation Evaluations and Rubrics* (pp. 78–81)—Forms and rubrics for teacher and student evaluation of extension project presentations.

Extension Projects

Getting Started Literature Extension Projects

Accordion Book: Choose three to five significant scenes from your book. Create an illustrated book that reveals the sequence of your book's story line. Include written descriptions: What is happening in this scene? Why is the scene important to you?

Bookmark: Create a bookmark featuring either your favorite character or the character you consider to be most significant in your book. Be sure to include the book title and author, as well as the character's name and portrait or illustration. Adaptation: On the back of the bookmark, explain why you selected your featured character.

Cube: Create a six-sided tagboard cube focusing on your favorite scenes, significant story events, or characters from your book.

Story Hat: Make a "newspaper hat" out of a piece of white butcher paper. At the top of the front side of the hat, write the name of your book and the author. Divide the front brim into three sections. In the first section, draw something that happened at the beginning of the book. In the middle section, draw something that happened in the middle of the book. In the last section, draw the problem of the story. Then, divide the brim on the back of your hat into two sections. In the first section, draw how the problem was solved. In the last section, draw something that happened at the end of your book.

More Complex Literature Extension Projects

ABC Book: Create an ABC book, focusing on key events, characters, ideas, and information from your book. This may work best as a group project since the book will have 26 pages, one for each letter of the alphabet.

CD Cover: Design both the front and back cover for a CD to capture the theme or spirit of your book. Be sure the name of the book, plus the title of the hit single appears on the front cover along with an appealing sketch or design. On the back, list the other songs from the CD, making sure they relate to the book and the characters' experiences.

Commemorative Stamp: Select a key character or scene, or focus on an important theme from your book, and develop a stamp to commemorate that character, scene, or theme. Include a picture, a selected phrase, and the stamp's value.

Jackdaw: A jackdaw is a collection of artifacts representing ideas, events, characters, and/or themes in your book. Create a jackdaw and build a display of these items. Label each artifact, sharing its importance to the book. You may also want to include a direct quotation from your book for some items.

Story Quilt: Create quilt squares that represent key aspects or characters in your book. Each quilt square needs to include an illustration and a written explanation. Select an important quote from your chapter and write it inside your quilt square. Include a border with a repeated design or symbol that represents a key idea from your chapter or scene. Mount the squares on a piece of butcher paper or connect the squares with yarn. This is a good group project since your quilt should have between 16 and 25 squares.

Extension Project Focus Questions

How does my project show what I have learned from the book?

In what ways does my project include information from my book?

In what ways did the extension project cause me to revisit the book?

In what ways did the extension project use diverse forms of response?

When someone views my project, what will they learn about my book?

How did my extension project help me see connections with other books, my experiences, or the curriculum?

These questions are used to guide students as they plan and evaluate extension projects.

Extension Projects

Book Projects and Genres

Each of these genres will be discussed in class prior to the homework assignment. Each type of response project will also be demonstrated in class so that your child is clear about the expectations. A rubric with the criteria for evaluation will be sent home for each project.

OCTOBER: Read a mystery
Draw cards to answer questions about your book (i.e., characters, setting your favorite part, etc.)

NOVEMBER: Read historical fiction or historical nonfiction
Make a story map.

DECEMBER: Read a book of poetry
Make a poster and memorize a poem.

JANUARY: Read a folktale, fairy tale, or collection of folktales or fairy tales
Make a game.

FEBRUARY: Read a nonfiction book
Write a book review for "Storyworks" magazine.

MARCH: Read a biography or autobiography
Dress as the main character or make a "jackdaw" display to tell about the person's life.

APRIL: Read a fiction book with an animal as the main character or a nonfiction book about an animal
Create the animal from any medium for our pet show.

MAY: Free Choice!
Read a genre of your choice and celebrate it in a format you have enjoyed this year or a new one you've created yourself. Do this one alone or with a friend.

Extension Projects

Nonfiction Book Project Letter

Dear Parents and Students,

Our book report format this month is to write a book review. Attached is a copy of a book review from *Storyworks*, a magazine that publishes children's work, plus a review that our class wrote today for practice. There are also good examples at the end of the television program, *Reading Rainbow*.

A review should include: (a) the title of the book, (b) the author and illustrator, (c) the publisher, (d) the date it was published, and (e) the number of pages. The review may also include a catchy beginning, why you liked (or disliked) the book, who you think might enjoy the book, unique features about the book, etc. You may also want to make a rating system and then rate your book (i.e., 5 stars, thumbs up, etc.).

Parents will probably need to help their child locate a book, find the name of the author, illustrator, publisher, and date published. The rest of the review your child should be able to do independently. We will be sending these reviews into *Storyworks Magazine*, so the reviews need to be typewritten (it's okay for an adult to do that) or neatly handwritten.

We would like students to read a nonfiction book this month. These can include how-to books, science and nature books, biographies, history, etc.

The due date is Thursday the 27th. Please let us know if you have any questions.

Sandy Figel and Donna Kerns

Extension Projects

Scoring Rubric for Nonfiction Book Report

Name: _____ Date: _____

Book Title: _____

Teacher's evaluation:

❒ Student was prepared to present report on due date

❒ Student read a nonfiction book

❒ Book review included title, author, illustrator, publisher, date published, and # of pages

❒ Review was neatly printed or typed

❒ Extra _____

Score: _____

4 Students exceeded criteria
3 Student met standard (4 of the criteria)
2 Student met 3 of the criteria
1 Student met only 1 or 2 of the criteria

Comments/Goals:

Student's Self-Evaluation:

❒ I was prepared on the due date

❒ I read a nonfiction book

❒ My book review had the title, author, illustrator, publisher, the date it was published, and the number of pages

❒ My review was neatly printed or typed

❒ Extra _____

My Score: _____

4 I did extra
3 I did all 4 of the things required
2 I did 3 of the things required
1 I only did 1 or 2 of the things required

Comments/Goals:

Extension Projects

Extension Planning Sheet

Name: _____   **Date:** _____

Title: _____   **Author:** _____

Reading extension project:

_____

Extension project partner(s):

_____

Book pages that will be used:

_____

Drafting Ideas:

Extension Celebration Plan

Literature Circle Members: _____

_____

Book Title: _____

We are going to:

_____

_____

_____

_____

We will need:

_____   _____

_____   _____

_____   _____

_____   _____

_____   _____

Extension Projects

Literature Circles Extension Plan

Name: _____   **Title:** _____

Project: _____

I am working on my project with: _____

_____

Here is a golden line I'll use in my project, from page: _____

_____

_____

_____

_____

I've chosen this project as the best way to show you what I know because:

_____

_____

_____

_____

_____

_____

Extension Projects

Extension Project Plan: Story Quilt

Name: _____   Book Title: _____

BORDER:

1. Color: _____

Explain why your group decided this color best represents your book:

_____

_____

_____

2. Design:

With your group, decide on three designs or symbols that will be repeated in your border. Draw them neatly in the box below.

```



```

Explain why these symbols or designs make sense for your book:

_____

_____

_____

_____

Response Project

My project is a _____

It is about a book called _____

_____

_____

I like my project because _____

_____

_____

_____

Extension Projects

Project Evaluation

Date: _____

Book Title and Author: _____

Members: _____

Project: _____

WHAT THINGS WENT WELL?

☐ We got along   ☐ Everyone helped

☐ We worked quietly   ☐ We discussed ideas

☐ We are proud of our project   ☐ We had fun

☐ We all participated in our
   presentation

_____

_____

_____

_____

_____

WHAT COULD HAVE GONE BETTER?

_____

_____

_____

_____

Response Project Self-Evaluation

Name: _____   Project: _____

Describe the process you went through as you created your project.

_____

_____

_____

_____

_____

How does your project show quality and effort?

_____

_____

_____

_____

How does this piece show what you have learned about the book?

_____

_____

_____

_____

What did you learn from creating this project?

_____

_____

_____

_____

Extension Projects

Response Project Evaluation

Name: _____

Date: _____

Title: _____

Project:

☐ ABC Book
☐ Commemorative Stamp
☐ CD Cover
☐ Main Idea Belt
☐ Accordion Book

Grading Criteria:

_____ Project illustrations are relevant to the story (20)

_____ Project includes information from or about the story (20)

_____ Time and effort (10)

_____ Neatness (10)

_____ Creativity (10)

_____ **Overall Grade**

_____ **Percentage**

Comments:

Response Project Evaluation

Name: _____

Date: _____

Title: _____

Project:

☐ ABC Book
☐ Commemorative Stamp
☐ CD Cover
☐ Main Idea Belt
☐ Accordion Book

Grading Criteria:

_____ Project illustrations are relevant to the story (20)

_____ Project includes information from or about the story (20)

_____ Time and effort (10)

_____ Neatness (10)

_____ Creativity (10)

_____ **Overall Grade**

_____ **Percentage**

Comments:

Extension Projects

Story Quilt Evaluation

Name: _____   **Date:** _____

Title: _____

SELF EVALUATION	TEACHER EVALUATION
___ **ILLUSTRATIONS (20)** • Includes border and main illustration • Illustrations relate to theme • Border includes symbols and colors	___ **ILLUSTRATIONS (20)** • Includes border and main illustration • Illustrations relate to theme • Border includes symbols and colors

___ **WRITTEN DESCRIPTION (20)**
(on back of quilt square)
• Quality of writing
   Discusses theme and explains illustrations
• Grammar
   Spelling
   Punctuation
   Sentence structure
	___ **WRITTEN DESCRIPTION (20)**
	(on back of quilt square)
	• Quality of writing
	   Discusses theme and explains illustrations
	• Grammar
	   Spelling
	   Punctuation
	   Sentence structure

___ **TIME AND EFFORT (5)** • Neatness • Details	___ **TIME AND EFFORT (5)** • Neatness • Details
___ **CREATIVITY (5)**	___ **CREATIVITY (5)**
___ **TOTAL POINTS (50)**	___ **TOTAL POINTS (50)**

In what ways does your quilt square represent the theme?

Extension Projects

Setting Pamphlet Evaluation

Name: _____ **Date:** _____

Title: _____

STUDENT SELF EVALUATION	TEACHER EVALUATION
COVER:	**COVER:**
___ Title (1)	___ Title (1)
___ Author (1)	___ Author (1)
___ Illustration (1)	___ Illustration (1)
INSIDE:	**INSIDE:**
___ One illustration per panel (4)	___ One illustration per panel (4)
___ One paragraph explaining each illustration (1)	___ One paragraph explaining each illustration (1)
PRESENTATION:	**PRESENTATION:**
___ Conventions (2)	___ Conventions (2)
___ Neat (1)	___ Neat (1)
___ Everything is done in ink (1)	___ Everything is done in ink (1)
___ Effort (1)	___ Effort (1)
___ Your name (1)	___ Your name (1)
___ **TOTAL POINTS (21)**	___ **TOTAL POINTS (21)**
COMMENTS:	**COMMENTS:**

Extension Projects

Response Project Rubric

Name: _____   **Date:** _____

Check the boxes that apply to this response project, then mark an "X" in the top bar to indicate approximate placement on a continuum. Use the back for comments: what you noticed as strengths and weaknesses, and what you found interesting and unique.

NOVICE	APPRENTICE	PRACTITIONER	EXPERT
☐ project does not convey meaning of book	☐ project partially communicates meaning of book	☐ project adequately communicates meaning of book	☐ project clearly communicates meaning of book
☐ no organization evident	☐ lacks organization	☐ generally organized	☐ well organized
☐ lacks appeal	☐ some visual appeal	☐ visually appealing to audience	☐ visually creative and artistic
☐ little attention to details	☐ slight attention to details	☐ strong attention to details	☐ thorough attention to details
☐ minimal response from audience	☐ may or may not draw audience to book	☐ project somewhat attracts audience to book	☐ convincingly draws audience to book

Comments:

Presentation Evaluation

Presenter: _____   **Date:** _____

1. Spoke loudly and clearly	1	2	3	4	5
2. Had good eye contact	1	2	3	4	5
3. Showed visual aids well	1	2	3	4	5
4. Looked practiced and organized	1	2	3	4	5
5. Had all the information and it made sense	1	2	3	4	5

Average score: _____

The best thing this presenter did was _____
_____

Presentation Evaluation

Presenter: _____   **Date:** _____

1. Spoke loudly and clearly	1	2	3	4	5
2. Had good eye contact	1	2	3	4	5
3. Showed visual aids well	1	2	3	4	5
4. Looked practiced and organized	1	2	3	4	5
5. Had all the information and it made sense	1	2	3	4	5

Average score: _____

The best thing this presenter did was _____
_____

Extension Projects

Two Stars and a Wish

Name: _____   **Project:** _____

Reviewer: _____   **Date:** _____

☆ _____

_____

_____

☆ _____

_____

_____

Wish: _____

_____

Two Stars and a Wish

Name: _____   **Project:** _____

Reviewer: _____   **Date:** _____

☆ _____

_____

_____

☆ _____

_____

_____

Wish: _____

_____

Copyright © 2001 Christopher-Gordon Publishers

Presentation Rubric

4 WOW! TERRIFIC!	• I spoke loudly all of the time. • I faced the audience all of the time. • I looked at the audience all of the time. • I was serious all of the time. • I followed along all of the time. • I knew when it was my turn all of the time. • I did my part well.
3 You've Got It!	• I spoke loudly most of the time. • I faced the audience most of the time. • I looked at the audience most of the time. • I was serious most of the time. • I followed along most of the time. • I knew when it was my turn most of the time. • I did my part well most of the time.
2 Not Yet	• I spoke loudly some of the time. • I faced the audience some of the time. • I looked at the audience some of the time. • I was serious some of the time. • I followed along some of the time. • I knew when it was my turn some of the time. • I did some of my part.
1 Try Again!	• I did not speak loudly. • I rarely faced the audience. • I rarely looked at the audience. • I was not serious. • I did not follow along. • I did not know when it was my turn. • I did not participate.

Extension Projects

Presentation Rubric

Name: _____   **Date:** _____

Check the boxes that apply to this presentation, then mark an "X" in the top bar to indicate approximate placement on a continuum. Use the back for comments: what you noticed as strengths and weaknesses, and what you found interesting and unique.

NOVICE	APPRENTICE	PRACTITIONER	EXPERT
☐ not prepared for presentation	☐ not fully prepared or rehearsed for presentation	☐ evidence of adequate preparation and rehearsal	☐ thoroughly prepared and rehearsed
☐ little eye contact with audience	☐ occasionally looks at audience	☐ eye contact with most of the audience most of the time	☐ eye contact engages all of the audience
☐ little voice inflection (too quiet, too loud, or monotone)	☐ occasional use of voice inflection and volume	☐ adequate use of voice inflection and volume	☐ skillful use of voice inflection, volume and expression

Comments:

Classroom Based Assessment

Extension Projects

Part 5

Families and Literature Circles

If our goal is to nurture life-long readers, then we hope that reading flourishes both inside and outside of school. In this section, we present sample letters from several classroom teachers suggesting how parents and other family members can help readers prepare for literature circle discussions at school. There is also a detailed explanation of how one teacher invites her students to participate in a literature circle at home with an adult before she begins her first literature circle unit in the classroom. Several of these letters were adapted from Christy Clausen's parent letter in *Literature Circles and Response* (p. 25).

Some teachers have started quarterly evening literature circles in which adults and children gather to discuss a book they have read together. You can find other suggestions for family book clubs in *The Mother-Daughter Book Club* (1997), written by Shireen Dodson.

Of course, you will want to adapt all of these ideas and letters to fit your structure, themes, grade level, groups of students, and the availability of adult or older student volunteers.

Teaching Suggestions

- *Family Letters* (pp. 84–87)—Four teachers' letters to families about how they can help children prepare for literature circles by reading and discussing literature circle books at home. You will want to adapt these for your grade level and structure. Notice how each teacher's letter reflects her focus and beliefs. You could also adapt these letters for adult or older student volunteers in your classroom.

- *Parent-Child Literature Circles Guidelines* (p. 88)—A description of literature circles at home.

- *Evening Book Clubs* (p. 92)—An explanation and introductory letter about an evening book club for families. Again, this format could be adapted for use with other adults or older student volunteers.

Literature Circles Family Letter: Sample #1

Dear Families of Room 1B:

Literature circles are now a regular part of our reading program. On Fridays, I will introduce the book choices. Students will then select a book and bring it home to read over the weekend. The literature discussion groups will meet on Mondays and Tuesdays. Students will be expected to write about their books in their Reading Response Folders. In addition, some centers for the week will contain book extensions based on these books.

Your child has selected a book from several choices related by theme. Remember that because your child has self selected this book, it may not be a book at his or her independent reading level. Please read the book with your child, reading to them if necessary. The students will then share selections from their books in their groups on Mondays. Eventually, the students will be leading the discussions of these books.

Here are some ways for you to read and discuss these books together in preparation for the group discussion on Monday:

• Please have your child read (or read to him or her) and talk about the story as you read. Talking about the book will enhance your child's understanding.

• Read the book a second time and note favorite passages. Have your child use "Post-it" notes to mark any pages that he or she would like to share and talk about in the group. What kinds of things should your child mark? Note places that are funny, interesting, puzzling (things he or she doesn't understand), or passages that relate to his or her life. Your child may want to mark a place where he or she notices the author's style, something about one of the characters, the main idea of the story, or certain details or illustrations.

• If possible, your child should be prepared to read the selected part(s) to the group. Our goal is that by the end of the year, all students will be participating in this manner.

• Send the book back to school on Monday with the pages marked.

Thank you for your support and assistance! I look forward to the many discussions this year which will expand and promote our love of reading.

Sincerely,

Vicki Yousoofian

Families and Literature Circles

Literature Circles Family Letter: Sample #2

Dear Families,

On Friday, each child will bring home a book he/she has chosen. Let your child read the book to you or read the book aloud together.

How to Prepare for Literature Circles at Home

1. Please have your child read (or read with him/her) and talk about the story as you read. Talking about books enhances your child's understanding, which is the main reason for reading!

2. Read the story once or twice each night. Good books are meant to be read again and again for enjoyment!

3. Have your child use the "Post-it" notes in the plastic book bag to mark any pages of interest that he/she would like to share and talk about in class. What kinds of things should your child mark? Your child may want to mark places in the book that are funny, interesting, puzzling (things he/she did not understand), or passages that relate to his/her life. Your child may want to mark a place where he/she notices the author's style, something about one of the characters, the main idea within the story, certain details, or the illustrations.

4. Send the book back on Monday with the pages marked with "Post-it" notes. We will talk about the book in literature groups on Monday. On the rest of the days, we will do a variety of activities pertaining to your child's chosen book.

Questions to Ask Your Child Before Reading
What do you think this story is going to be about? How can you tell?
What do you think is going to happen next?
How do you think the story is going to end?

Questions to Ask Your Child During or After Reading
Have you ever felt like any of the characters in this book?
How are you like or different from the characters in this story?
Does this remind you of anything you've done before?

Sincerely,

Diana Kastner

Families and Literature Circles

Literature Circles Family Letter: Sample #3

Dear Families,

Your child is bringing home his/her literature circle book to read at home. Please read it with your child at least once or twice and help him/her mark parts for discussion. We will discuss the book together in class in small groups. It is important that the book comes back to school by Wednesday morning for our discussion time.

Please keep in mind that this book is not necessarily at your child's independent reading level. Picture books can have some really difficult words! Literature circles are just one part of our reading program. Reading instruction takes place in many other ways in our classroom. The purpose of literature circles is to expose children to good literature, promote thoughtful reading, and teach students how to have a literary discussion.

Thanks for your participation! Please let me know if you have any questions.

Sincerely,

Sandy Figel

Literature Circles Family Letter: Sample #4

Dear Families,

Your second grader is about to begin a themed literature unit called, "Seeing Community Through Another's Eyes." The purpose of this unit is to expand student thinking about the concept of community. Our previous social studies unit has given us the background knowledge that we will need to explore the diversity of community life on our planet with an understanding of the importance community plays in the lives of the people who live and work in a shared environment. A selection of children's literature will be used as a vehicle for discussions about different kinds of communities and the characteristics that make each one valuable to its inhabitants.

Throughout this unit your second grader will:

- Demonstrate an appreciation of diverse communities and the characteristics that make a community valuable to its inhabitants.
- Learn and practice new skills and strategies to become stronger and more confident readers.
- Participate in literature circles in order to share and gain information about themed literature.

Throughout this unit, students will participate in activities designed to introduce, teach, and review the information that they will need in order to meet the learning targets described above. The following activities will provide opportunities for the assessment of student learning:

- Reading themed literature.
- Participation in literature circle discussions.
- Journal writing in response to theme-related prompts.
- Creation of extension projects that will allow students to summarize their learning through reading, writing, and the creation of artwork.

The theme, "Seeing Community Through Another's Eyes" provides an opportunity for students to consider the perspectives and experiences of others. I invite all of you to share your own community experiences with our class as we investigate the diversity of our global community.

Please feel free to contact me with any questions, concerns, or suggestions.

Sincerely,

Elizabeth Bentley

Parent-Child Literature Circles Guidelines

We would like to begin this school year with a parent-child home literature circle. Many of you already read with your children on an on-going basis; and research shows that such shared reading continues to be highly valuable, even long after children become independent readers. This is especially true if parent-child reading includes dialogue about what is read. In this assignment, we hope to provide a flexible structure that encourages your child to become engaged in a dialogue with you about a book. In the process, your child will be enhancing his/her comprehension skills and will be learning more of the discussion skills necessary to participate in the classroom literature circles that will be a part of his/her third grade (and beyond!) experience.

BOOK CHOICE

We would like parents to choose a book to be read with their child. This can be any book you think your child would enjoy and may be a book beyond your child's independent reading level if you would like to read it aloud. Any chapter book may be chosen, but your choice may be determined by thinking of a book you believe your child may enjoy but may not necessarily find on his/her own, or a memorable book you recall reading when you were a child of similar age. If you need any assistance choosing books, please ask us! We can share a list of books being read by class members and parents, and those who have not yet found a book may find the list helpful in making their choice. When you have chosen a book, it would be helpful if you let us know your choice.

Format

Reading: After you have chosen a book, we would like you to begin reading with your child. This reading can be accomplished in the way that you and your child find most comfortable. For example, some parent/child partnerships may choose to read the book aloud. Either the parent may read aloud, or the parent and child may alternate. Other partnerships may choose to have two book copies and read the book independently. Please discuss and plan with your child, accomplishing the reading in a way which best suits you.

Discussion: Our hope is that this shared reading experience will lead to discussion. Please do not feel you need to "teach" the book. Rather, we hope you and your child have the opportunity to discuss the book in a natural and comfortable manner. While what you and your child talk about will be influenced by the book you read, here are some ideas about how you can begin and keep a discussion going:

You can model responding to issues and ideas. Explain your own genuine reaction to events in the book. If appropriate, make a connection to your life.

- "I enjoyed this part because . . . "

- "This reminds me of when I was that age . . . "

- "This character/situation makes me think of . . . "

- Ask your child a question about what they think. You may ask them to predict what might happen next, or to think about what they would do in a similar situation.

- "I was surprised by . . . (at a turn of events). I wonder what will happen next? What do you think?"

- "What would you do if . . . ?"

These are only ideas. Please know that as long as you and your child are talking and the discussion is genuine, you are helping your child to be a more thoughtful reader!

Journaling: Some families have found it valuable to keep a journal as they read. Others have found journaling cumbersome and overwhelming. Please decide what is most helpful and reasonable for your family. If you would like to consider keeping a journal, these are some options:

- Some parents and children in the past have had separate journals. After reading a mutually agreed upon portion of the book, each has written a response and then met together to share. (This is quite similar to what we do in class literature circles.) They then plan how far to read before the next meeting.

- Other parents and children have shared a journal, passing it back and forth to each other, and responding to what the other has written. In this case, much of the discussion was in fact written.

- Still others have met together primarily to discuss what has been read and have recorded the main or most important points of the discussion.

TIMELINE

Book Choice: We would like you to choose your book sometime before October 12. By October 12, we would like to know which book you have chosen. I would like parent to choose the book for this assignment. Please consider any input that children give yo and consider their interests, attention span, reading level, etc. If you are doing this assignment as a "read aloud," it will allow you to choose a book above your child's independent reading level. This assignment can also be an opportunity to expose children to books that they may not find on their own. Some parents in the past have enjoyed reading a book they remembered from their childhood (some even had old, worn copies!). Some have also arranged to read the same book a classmate is reading.

Attached is a note you can send in notifying us of your choice. If you decide earlier, please let us know and we will share a list of books the students will be reading. Remember to let us know if you need help making a choice.

Reading and Discussion: We would like students to begin reading the week of October 12. If you have a long book and have chosen before this time, please feel free to begin reading and discussing earlier. We would like you and your child to keep some record of discussions using one of the formats discussed above. If you are reading independently using two copies of the book, you will want to mutually decide how far to read before meeting for your next discussion or journal exchange.

Reading Completion: We would like the reading of books to be completed over Thanksgiving weekend or earlier *(by November 29).*

Culminating Activity: As a culminating activity, we would like each student and parent partnership to write a *book talk*. The book talk includes:

- Name and author of book.

- Genre of book.

- How this book was chosen for this project (parents chose these books for the most part but WHY did they choose this particular book for their child?).

- Did you like the book? (Parent's and child's opinion may vary!) Why or why not? Explain!

- Tell a little bit about the book, but be sure it is brief and does not tell the entire story. Try to tell enough that your listeners might become interested (whet their appetite!) but have to read it themselves to find out what happens! Leave them hanging!

- Is there someone you recommend this book to? If so, why do you think they may enjoy it?

(We will teach students this format and send it home again before the due date.)

CELEBRATION

We will be inviting students and parents who are able to attend to a celebration of reading the morning of Thursday, December 2. During this celebration, students and their parents will share their book and experiences with others who have read the same genre or type of book. (For example, groups who have read mysteries will meet together.) Although we would love for as many parents as possible to attend, students who come without parents will be able to share both their journal (if they chose to do one) and book talk.

Finally, we know this is a different type of assignment. While we have found it to be a very valuable experience, we know you may have questions. Please feel free to ask! Keep in mind the most valuable part of this experience will be sharing with your child. If you share your own genuine responses in the course of reading and discussing, you will have accomplished a great deal. Feel free to allow your discussion to "go off the page" and encourage your child to connect the book to his/her own experiences and observations. We truly hope this is a fun, relaxing experience that you and your child enjoy.

Sincerely,

Cindy Flegenheimer and Linda Horn

Evening Book Clubs

Purpose

The Evening Book Club was designed to allow families to become involved with their child as a reader. Because literature circles are an integral part of my classroom, family support is crucial. I wanted to invite families into our reading community. I also wanted to have the children see the influence and impact of reading in the lives of adults.

Another key to the success of the Book Club was the involvement of our librarian. She contributed wonderful insights about books and authors and asked great questions at our meetings. We have also been fortunate to have community members also attend, such as our county librarian.

Organization

Early in the fall, I gathered with families and children who were interested in participating in an Evening Book Club. Together, we brainstormed book titles and I shared with them my goals. We chose a title, set a date to discuss the book, and began reading. I prepared a small activity in advance. As adults and children entered the room, this activity broke the ice and provided a springboard into our discussion. I shared a chart of the "Tools for Discussion" that students use in class to foster a respectful discussion group. Then we plunged into our conversation. After 45 minutes, I wrapped up the discussion and shared possible titles for the next meeting. We chose a book and set a date for the next Evening Book Club.

Book Choices

I encourage both adults and students to bring suggestions for book titles they would like to read. I base my selections on several criteria: content/interest, connections to in-class literature circle titles, and book availability. Here is a list of the books we have used this year:

Tuck Everlasting by Natalie Babbit

From the Mixed-up Files of Mrs. Basil E. Frankweiler by E. L. Konigsburg

Yolonda's Genius by Carol Fenner

Roll of Thunder, Hear My Cry by Mildred Taylor

The Giver by Lois Lowry

Dear Parents,

Now that the school year is underway and we have all fallen back into our "school routine," I wanted to let you know about the evening book club. I understand that many of you were not able to attend the planning meeting earlier this month and because I wanted to get started reading, I have made the book choice for this first meeting. The book is *Tuck Everlasting* by Natalie Babbit. I hope that after our first gathering, the book choice will be a collaborative decision.

Tuck Everlasting is a fabulous book about a young girl who struggles with her family life and the friendship she develops with the Tuck family. The Tucks live in a nearby forest and have drunk from a fountain that prevents them from dying. I think you will find that the issues in this book will lead to wonderful discussions.

There are multiple copies of this book here at school and I would be happy to lend a copy to you and your child. It can also be found at your local library or bookstore. Whether the book is read independently or together, I know you will both come to the meeting with some great questions and ideas to share with the group.

I have scheduled the discussion about this book for _____ from 6:30–7:30 p.m. If you will be participating in the evening book club that will be reading *Tuck Everlasting*, please send the bottom portion of this letter back to school with your child. I would like to have an estimate of the number of families who will be attending in order to better plan for October's discussion.

I will have snacks and beverages to share and look forward to this fantastic opportunity to share the love of literature with you and your child. Please feel free to contact me any time via email or phone if you have questions.

Sincerely

Sarah Dunkin

☐   Yes, my child and I would like to be a part of the evening book club for the month of October. I plan to attend on _____ to join others in the discussion of *Tuck Everlasting*.

☐   Yes, I would appreciate borrowing *Tuck Everlasting* from the school.

☐   No, I don't need to borrow a book.

Part 6

References

Blecher, Sharon, & Jaffee, Kathy. (1998). *Weaving in the arts: Widening the learning circle.* Portsmouth, NH: Heinemann.

Daniels, Harvey. (1994). *Literature circles: Voice and choice in the student-centered classroom.* York, ME: Stenhouse.

Dodson, Shirley. (1997). *The mother-daughter book club.* New York: HarperCollins.

Duthie, Christine. (1996). *True stories: Nonfiction literacy in the primary classroom.* York, ME: Stenhouse.

Fox, Mem. (1993). *Radical reflections: Passionate opinions on teaching, learning, and living.* San Diego, CA: Harcourt Brace.

Gambrell, Linda, & Almasi, Janice. (Eds.) (1997). *Lively discussions! Fostering engaged reading.* Newark, DE: International Reading Association.

Hagerty, Patricia. (1992). *Readers' workshop: Real reading.* New York: Scholastic.

Harris, Violet. (Ed.). (1993). *Teaching multicultural literature in grades K–8.* Norwood, MA: Christopher-Gordon.

Harste, Jerome, Short, Kathy, & Burke, Carolyn. (1988). *Creating classrooms for authors: The reading-writing connection.* Portsmouth, NH: Heinemann.

Harvey, Stephanie. (1998). *Nonfiction matters: Reading, writing, and research in grades 3–8.* York, ME: Stenhouse.

Hill, Bonnie Campbell, Ruptic, Cynthia, & Norwick, Lisa. (1998). *Classroom based assessment.* Norwood, MA: Christopher-Gordon.

Hill, Bonnie Campbell, & Ruptic, Cynthia. (1994). *Practical aspects of authentic assessment: Putting the pieces together.* Norwood, MA: Christopher-Gordon.

Hill, Bonnie Campbell, Johnson, Nancy J., & Schlick Noe, Katherine L. (Eds.) (1995). *Literature circles and response.* Norwood, MA: Christopher-Gordon.

Holland, Kathleen, Hungerford, Rachael, & Ernst, Shirley. (1993). *Journeying: Children responding to literature.* Portsmouth, NH: Heinemann.

Moss, Joy. (1994). *Using literature in the middle grades: A thematic approach.* Norwood, MA: Christopher-Gordon.

Parsons, Les. (1990). *Response journals.* Portsmouth, NH: Heinemann.

Peterson, Ralph, & Eeds, Maryann. (1990). *Grand conversations: Literature groups in action.* New York: Scholastic.

Rhodes, Lynn. (1993). *Literacy assessment: A handbook of instruments.* Portsmouth, NH: Heinemann.

Rief, Linda. (1999). *Vision and voice: Extending the literacy spectrum.* Portsmouth, NH: Heinemann.

Rief, Linda. (1991). *Seeking diversity: Language arts with adolescents.* Portsmouth, NH: Heinemann.

Roser, Nancy, & Martinez, Miriam. (1995). *Book talk and beyond: Children and teachers respond to literature.* Newark, DE: International Reading Association.

Routman, Regie. (1991, 1994). *Invitations: Changing as teachers and learners K–12.* Portsmouth, NH: Heinemann.

Routman, Regie. (2000). *Conversations: Strategies for teaching, learning, and evaluating.* Portsmouth, NH: Heinemann.

Samway, Katharine Davies, & Whang, Gail. (1995). *Literature study circles in a multicultural classroom.* York, ME: Stenhouse.

Schlick Noe, Katherine L., & Johnson, Nancy J. (1999). *Getting started with literature circles.* Norwood, MA: Christopher-Gordon.

Short, Kathy. (1997). *Literature as a way of knowing.* York, ME: Stenhouse.

Short, Kathy, & Pierce, Kathryn Mitchell. (Eds.) (1990). *Talking about books: Creating literate communities.* Portsmouth, NH: Heinemann.

Wollman-Bonilla, Julie. (1991). *Response journals: Inviting students to think and write about literature.* New York: Scholastic.

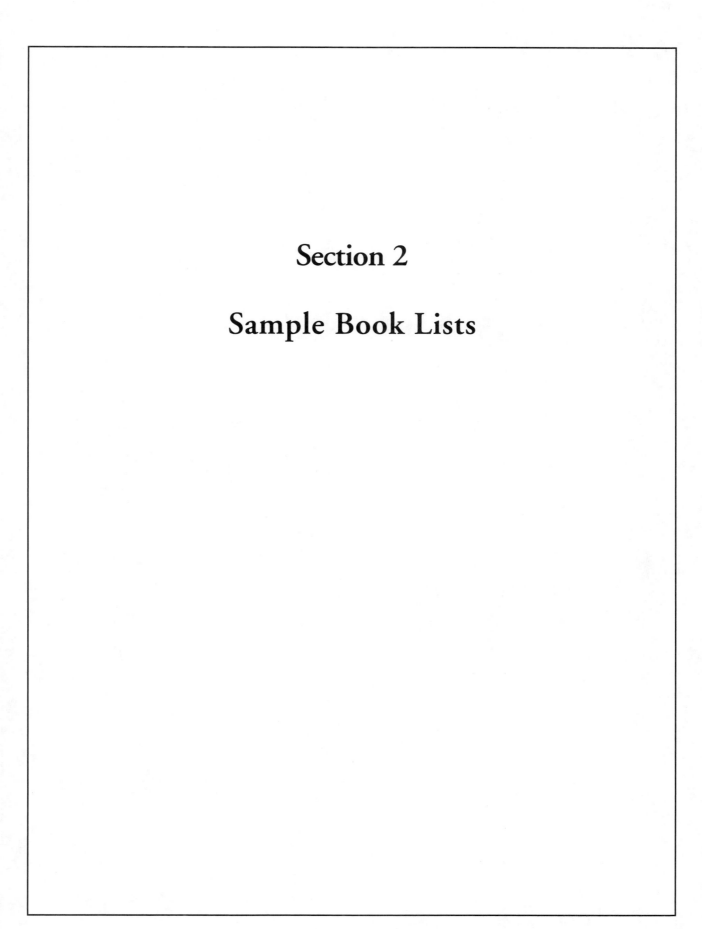

Section 2

Sample Book Lists

Sample Book Lists

Many teachers have asked us for sample lists of books that teachers use successfully in literature circles. Teachers organize their literature circles in many ways, including by theme (courage), genre (fantasy), or time period (civil war). We organized the sample book lists into these three categories. In addition, you may want to organize literature circles around the work of a particular author. We have included suggestions for Author/Illustrator studies.

We categorized the book lists into three broad grade level ranges: primary, intermediate, and upper intermediate/middle school. This organization makes sense for several reasons. We were reluctant to provide lists by grade level, since there are always a range of reading abilities and interests in any one class. We were also aware of a tendency to label a book as a "fifth grade novel" or a "second grade book"—thereby limiting its use in other classrooms. In addition, students in multiage classrooms span several grade levels. Based on your particular group of students, you may need to include book choices from more than one list.

We blended many teachers' lists that had similar themes or book choices, adding titles of our own favorite books for literature circles. We hope that these sample lists will help you create your own book sets. Of course, your lists will vary from year to year, depending on your particular group of students, classroom topics and themes, and your students' interests.

We have included a large number of books designated as young adult. These can be found in the lists for upper intermediate/middle school and contain more mature subject matter and possibly more challenging language. In addition, we have listed picture books for older readers that may be too challenging in vocabulary and content for younger students. Your best guide for using any of the titles in these lists is to get the book in your hands and judge it for yourself.

Book List Format

Every book listed in the Sample Books Lists is also included in the database on the accompanying CD-ROM. The format of each book (e.g., picture book or chapter book) is identified in the database by the abbreviations listed below. The following section provides a brief definition of each book format.

PB = Picture Book: Illustrations support or extend the text. Picture books are generally of a vocabulary and interest level appropriate for primary grade readers. Picture Books can also be used effectively across the grade levels.

PBOR = Picture Book Older Readers: Illustrations accompany text to support or extend the book. Includes more challenging vocabulary or content intended for older readers. Picture Books for Older Readers can be used effectively across grade levels depending on students' abilities and interests.

ER = Early Reader: Illustrations on every page or every other page accompany text in limited chapters. Early Reader books serve as a transition from picture books to chapter books for primary grade readers.

EC = Easy Chapter Book: Illustrations are limited as written content becomes more dominant. Easy Chapter Books are flexible in use across grade levels, offering more in-depth content for younger readers, as well as shorter, more accessible text for older readers.

CH = Chapter Book: Books organized by chapters; appropriate for independent readers in the intermediate and middle school grades, and for capable readers in the primary grades.

YA = Young Adult: Chapter books with more challenging vocabulary and/or more mature content appropriate for older readers.

Using the Book Lists

You may want to begin by looking over the lists at your approximate teaching level. We suggest that you also refer to the other grade levels for books that might meet the needs of particular students. At the Primary level, we have included picture books, early readers, easy chapter books, and chapter books. Primary grade teachers looking for more challenging picture books and chapter books will find them in the Intermediate Book Lists. At the Intermediate level, most of the books listed are picture books for older readers and chapter books. Teachers may want to refer to the Primary Book Lists for easier picture books and chapter books. Upper Intermediate/Middle School teachers may want to select books from all three lists to meet the needs of a wide range of readers.

Sample Book Lists p. 103

Sample book lists by theme, genre, and time period. These lists are organized by level: Primary grades, Intermediate grades, and Upper Intermediate/Middle School.

Author Studies and References p. 163

Suggestions for author studies as a focus for literature circles or as inquiry studies. We also include a list of books about authors and illustrators.

Professional Resources and Web Sites p. 173

Lists of professional books and web sites about literature circles and publishers' phone numbers and web site addresses.

Levels

Part 1: Primary
Part 2: Intermediate
Part 3: Upper Intermediate/Middle School

Themes

1. Reaching Out to Others/Friendship
2. Family Issues
3. Generations Learning from One Another
4. Challenges
5. Courage
6. Standing Up for Your Beliefs
7. Justice
8. Survival
9. Respecting Nature
10. Caring for Animals

Genres

1. Fiction (FIC)
2. Historical Fiction (HF)
3. Biography (BIO)
4. Mystery (MYS)
5. Fantasy (FAN)
6. Science Fiction (SF)
7. Traditional Literature (TL)
8. Nonfiction (NF)
9. Poetry (POE)

Time Periods (Historical Fiction and Nonfiction)

1. Looking into the Ancient Past
2. Middle Ages and Renaissance
3. Early Colonial
4. Revolutionary War
5. Immigration and New Beginnings
6. Westward Expansion
7. Slavery and the American Civil War
8. Gold Rush
9. Turn of the Century
10. Women's Rights Movement
11. Great Depression
12. World War II
13. Japanese Internment
14. Civil Rights Movement
15. Conflict in Vietnam and Southeast Asia
16. Contemporary Challenges in Other Countries

Part 1

Primary Book Lists

See also Intermediate Book Lists for more challenging picture books and chapter books that would be appropriate for some primary grade readers.

Themes

Theme 1. Reaching Out to Others/Friendship

Picture Books
Angel Child, Dragon Child by Michelle Maria Surat
An Angel for Solomon Singer by Cynthia Rylant
Arctic Stories by Michael Arvaarluk Kusugak
Chester's Way by Kevin Henkes
Don't Need Friends by Carolyn Crimi
Good Luck, Mrs. K! by Louise Borden
Horace and Morris but Mostly Delores by James Howe
Ira Sleeps Over by Bernard Waber
Just Kids: Visiting a Class for Children with Special Needs by E. B. Senisi
Let's Talk About It: Extraordinary Friends by Fred Rogers
Lottie's New Friend by Petra Mathers
Miss Rumphius by Barbara Cooney
Mrs. Katz and Tush by Patricia Polacco
Officer Buckle and Gloria by Peggy Rathmann
Old Henry by Joan Blos
The Old Woman Who Named Things by Cynthia Rylant
Ruby the Copycat by Peggy Rathmann
Sam Johnson and the Blue Ribbon Quilt by Lisa Campbell Ernst
The Shy Little Girl by Phyllis Krasilovsky
Sing to the Stars by Mary Brigid Barrett
Somebody Loves You, Mr. Hatch by Eileen Spinelli
Stellaluna by Janelle Cannon
Swimmy by Leo Lionni
Uncle Willie and the Soup Kitchen by Dianne DiSalvo Ryan
Yoko by Rosemary Wells

Picture Books for Older Readers
Jingle Dancer by Cynthia Leitich Smith
When Willard Met Babe Ruth by Donald Hall

Early Readers
Frog and Toad Together by Arnold Lobel (series)
George and Martha by James Marshall (series)
The Golly Sisters Go West by Betsy Byars
Henry and Mudge by Cynthia Rylant (series)
Mouse Tales by Arnold Lobel

Mr. Putter and Tabby by Cynthia Rylant (series)
Next Spring an Oriole by Gloria Whelan
Poppleton by Cynthia Rylant (series)

Easy Chapter Books
Ant Plays Bear by Betsy Byars
Esio Trot by Roald Dahl
The Final Game by William Roy Brownridge
Jacob Two-Two and the Dinosaur by Mordecai Richler
A Lion to Guard Us by Clyde Robert Bulla
Marvin Redpost: Alone in His Teacher's House by Louis Sachar (series)
Owen Foote, Frontiersman by Stephanie Greene (series)
Stay Away from Simon by Carol Carrick

Chapter Books
Charlotte's Web by E. B. White
Stuart Little by E. B. White

Theme 2. Family Issues

Picture Books
All the Places to Love by Patricia MacLachlan
Allison by Allen Say
Anna's Special Present by Yoriko Tsutsui
At the Crossroads by Rachel Isadora
Boundless Grace by Mary Hoffman
The Boy Who Wanted a Family by Shirley Gordon
A Chair for My Mother by Vera B. Williams
Cherries and Cherry Pits by Vera B. Williams
Clarice Bean, That's Me by Lauren Child
Erandi's Braids by Antonio Hernandez Madrigal
Everett Anderson's Goodbye by Lucille Clifton
Far Away Home by Jane Kurtz
Going Home by Eve Bunting
Henry's Baby by Mary Hoffman
How My Parents Learned to Eat by Ina Friedman
It's My Birthday, Too! by Lynne Jonell
Jamela's Dress by Niki Daly
Julius, Baby of the World by Kevin Henkes
Koala Lou by Mem Fox
Mama One, Mama Two by Patricia MacLachlan
Max's Dragon Shirt by Rosemary Wells
Peter's Chair by Ezra Jack Keats
The Relatives Came by Cynthia Rylant
A Screaming Kind of Day by Rachna Gilmore
The Terrible Thing That Happened at Our House by Marge Blaine
Through Moon and Stars and Night Sky by Ann Turner
Tight Times by Barbara Shook Hazen
Weird Parents by Audrey Wood
When Sopie Gets Angry—Really, Really Angry by Molly Bang
William's Doll by Charlotte Zolotow
Youn Hee & Me by C. S. Adler
Zelda and Ivy by Laura McGee Kvasnosky

Picture Books for Older Readers
My Ol' Man by Patricia Polacco
My Rotten Red Headed Older Brother by Patricia Polacco
The Patchwork Quilt by Valerie Flournoy

Easy Chapter Books
26 Fairmount Avenue by Tomie dePaola
A Bargain for Frances by Russell Hoban (series)
Here We All Are by Tomie dePaola
Josie to the Rescue by Marilyn Singer
Koya DeLaney and the Good Girl Blues by Eloise Greenfield
Little Sister, Big Sister by Pat Brisson
Mister and Me by Kimberly Willis Holt
My Brother, Ant by Betsy Byars
The One in the Middle is the Green Kangaroo by Judy Blume
The Pain and the Great One by Judy Blume
The Stories Julian Tells by Ann Cameron (series)

Theme 3a. Generations Learning from One Another

Picture Books
Abuela by Arthur Dorros
Abuela's Weave by Omar Castaneda
Always My Dad by Sharon Dennis Wyeth
Aunt Flossie's Hats and Crab Cakes Later by Elizabeth Fitzgerald Howard
Back Home by Gloria Pinkney
Basket Moon by Mary Lyn Ray
The Bee Tree by Patricia Polacco
Big Moon Tortilla by Joy Cowley
A Birthday Basket for Tia by Pat Mora
Down the Winding Road by Angela Johnson
Fox Song by Joseph Bruchac
From Miss Ida's Porch by Sandra Belton
Grandaddy and Janetta by Helen Griffith
Grandaddy's Place by Helen Griffith
Granddaddy's Street Songs by Monalisa Degross
Grandfather's Lovesong by Reeve Lindbergh
Grandma According to Me by Karen Magnuson Beil
Grandpa's Face by Eloise Greenfield
Grandpa's Song by Tony Johnston
I Have an Olive Tree by Eve Bunting
Just Right Stew by Karen English
Laura Charlotte by Kathryn Galbraith
Liliana's Grandmothers by Leyla Torres
Miz Berlin Walks by Jane Yolen
My Grandma Leonie by Bijou le Tord
My Grandson Lew by Charlotte Zolotow
Nana Upstairs, Nana Downstairs by Tomie de Paola
Now One Foot, Now the Other by Tomie de Paola
The Old, Old Man and the Very Little Boy by Kristine Franklin
Our Granny by Margaret Wild
The Sunday Outing by Gloria Pinkney

Three Cheers for Catherine the Great by Cari Best
Through Grandpa's Eyes by Patricia MacLachlan
Thundercake by Patricia Polacco
Tom by Tomie dePaola
The Two of Them by Aliki
The Wednesday Surprise by Eve Bunting
When I Am Old with You by Angela Johnson
Wilfrid Gordon McDonald Partridge by Mem Fox

Early Readers
Grandmas at Bat by Emily Arnold McCully (series)

Easy Chapter Books
Gus and Grandpa and Show-and-Tell by Claudia Mills (series)

Theme 3b. Generations Learning From One Another (Quilts)

Picture Books
The Keeping Quilt by Patricia Polacco
Luka's Quilt by Georgia Guback
The Patchwork Quilt by Valerie Flournoy
The Quilt Story by Tony Johnston
Selina and the Bear Paw Quilt by Barbara Smucker

Easy Chapter Books
The Canada Geese Quilt by Natalie Kinsey-Warnock
The Josefina Story Quilt by Eleanor Coerr

Theme 4. Challenges

Picture Books
Angel Child, Dragon Child by Michelle Maria Surat
Amazing Grace by Mary Hoffman
Amelia's Road by Linda Jacobs Altman
Birdie's Lighthouse by Deborah Hopkinson
The Blizzard's Robe by Robert Sabuda
Chrysanthemum by Kevin Henkes
Danny and the Kings by Susan Cooper
Fly Away Home by Eve Bunting
The Gadget War by Ann Douglas
The Glorious Flight by Alice Provensen and Martin Provensen
Hide and Seek by Michael Arvaarluk Kusugak
Hue Boy by Rita Phillips Mitchell
I Hate English! by Ellen Levine
Jamaica and the Substitute Teacher by Jaunita Havill
The Leaving Morning by Angela Johnson
Leo the Late Bloomer by Jose Aruego
Lilly's Purple Plastic Purse by Kevin Henkes
Moses Goes to School by Isaac Millman
Moss Pillows by Rosemary Wells
Night Golf by William Miller
The Night the Iguana Left Home by Megan McDonald
Old Henry by Joan Blos
Owen by Kevin Henkes

Rainbow Tulip by Pat Mora
Shadow Story by Nancy Willard
Space Travellers by Margaret Wild
The Sunday Outing by Gloria Pinkney
Sylvester and the Magic Pebble by William Steig
The Tenth Good Thing about Barney by Judith Viorst
Vera's First Day of School by Vera Rosenberry

Early Readers
Mr. Putter and Tabby Pick the Pears by Cynthia Rylant (series)
Snow Walker by Margaret and Charles Wetterer

Easy Chapter Books
Aldo Applesauce by Johanna Hurwitz
The Chalk Box Kid by Clyde Robert Bulla
Gloria's Way by Ann Cameron
Howie Bowles, Secret Agent by Kate Banks (series)
Keep the Lights Burning, Abbie by Connie and Peter Roop
Molly's Pilgrim by Barbara Cohen
Morgy Makes His Move by Maggie Lewis
Owen Foote, Frontiersman by Stephanie Green (series)
The Skates of Uncle Richard by Carol Fenner
Stone Fox by John Reynolds Gardiner

Theme 5. Courage

Picture Books
Belinda's Hurricane by Elizabeth Winthrop
The Buffalo Jump by Peter Roop
Doctor De Soto by William Steig
Flight: The Journey of Charles Lindbergh by Robert Burleigh
Follow the Drinking Gourd by Jeanette Winter
The Girl Who Loved Wild Horses by Paul Goble
Lon Po Po: A Red Riding Hood Tale from China by Ed Young
Mole's Hill: A Woodland Tale by Lois Ehlert
Nessa's Fish by Nancy Luenn
Redcoats and Petticoats by Katherine Kirkpatrick
The Twister by Darleen Bailey Beard

Early Readers
Sir Small and the Dragonfly by Jane O'Connor

Easy Chapter Books
The Drinking Gourd by Ferdinand Monjo
Thunder at Gettysburg by Patricia Gauch

Theme 6. Standing Up for Your Beliefs

[See Intermediate]

Theme 7. Justice

[See Intermediate]

Theme 8. Survival

[See Intermediate]

Theme 9. Respecting Nature

Picture Books
Arctic Memories by Normee Ekoomiak
Butterfly House by Eve Bunting
The Great Kapok Tree by Lynne Cherry
Letting Swift River Go by Jane Yolen
Maria's Comet by Deborah Hopkinson
Out of the Ocean by Debra Frasier
Owl Moon by Jane Yolen
Prince William by Gloria Rand and Ted Rand
Rain Forest Secrets by Arthur Dorros
Song for an Ancient Forest by Nancy Luenn
The Storm by Kathy Henderson
The Sun, The Wind, and the Rain by Lisa Westberg Peters
The Twister by Darleen Bailey Beard

Easy Chapter Books
Hill of Fire by Thomas Lewis

Theme 10. Caring for Animals

Picture Books
Crab Moon by Ruth Horowitz
Dolphin's First Day: The Story of a Bottlenose Dolphin by Kathleen Weidner Zoehfeld
The Emperor's Egg by Martin Jenkins
Flute's Journey: The Life of a Wood Thrush by Lynne Cherry
How to Babysit an Orangutan by Tara Darling and Kathy Darling
How to Talk to Your Cat by Jean Craighead George
How to Talk to Your Dog by Jean Craighead George
My Puppy is Born by Joanna Cole
Nights of the Pufflings by Bruce McMillan
Real Live Monsters by Ellen Schecter
The Red-Eyed Tree Frog by Joy Cowley
Scruffy – A Wolf Finds His Place in the Pack by Jim Brandenburg
The Tenth Good Thing about Barney by Judith Viorst
Toby the Tabby Kitten by Colleen Stanley Bare
Wilderness Cat by Natalie Kinsey-Warnock

Early Readers
Sam the Sea Cow by Francine Jacobs

Easy Chapter Books
The Amazing Panda Adventure by John Wilcox and Steven Alldredge
Andy Bear: A Polar Cub Grows Up at the Zoo by Ginny Johnston and Judy Cutchins
Buddy, The First Seeing Eye Dog by Eva Moore
Dancing with Manatees by Faith McNulty
Ibis: A True Whale Tale by John Himmelman
Not My Dog by Colby Rodowsky
Outside Dog by Charlotte Pomerantz
Sable by Karen Hesse
The True Story of Balto: The Bravest Dog Ever by Natalie Standiford
The True Story of Corky, the Blind Sea Cow by Georgeanne Irvine

Genres

Genre 1. Fiction
[No Book List]

Genre 2. Historical Fiction
[See Time Period]

Genre 3a. Biography (Famous Artists)

Picture Books
A Bird or Two: A Story about Henri Matisse by Bijou Le Tord
Diego by Jonah Winter
My Name is Georgia by Jeanette Winter
The Starry Night by Neil Waldman

Picture Books for Older Readers
Getting to Know the World's Greatest Artists by Mike Venezia (series)
    Mary Cassatt
    Salvador Dali
    Da Vinci
    Paul Gauguin
    Michelangelo
    Monet
    Georgia O'Keefe
    Picasso
    Rembrant
    Van Gogh
Story Painter: The Life of Jacob Lawrence by John Dugglesby

Genre 3b. Biography (Famous Musicians)
[See also Intermediate]

Picture Books
Sebastian: A Book About Bach by Jeanette Winter

Picture Books for Older Readers
Getting to Know the World's Greatest Composers by Mike Venezia (series)
    George Gershwin
    Wolfgang Amadeus Mozart

Genre 4. Mystery

Picture Books
Miss Nelson is Missing by Harry Allard
The Mystery of King Karfu by Doug Cushman
Tough Cookie by David Wisniewski

Early Readers
Aunt Eater Loves a Mystery by Doug Cushman (series)
The Mystery of the Missing Dog by Elizabeth Levy (series)

Easy Chapter Books
Cam Jansen by David Adler (series)
Flatfoot Fox and the Case of the Missing Eye by Eth Clifford (series)

The Mystery of the Tooth Gremlin by Bonnie Graves
Nate the Great by Marjorie Weinman Sharmat (series)
Wild Willie and King Kyle, Detectives by Barbara Joosse

Genre 5a. Fantasy

Picture Books
Abiyoyo by Pete Seeger
The Dragon's Pearl by Julie Lawson
The Dream Collector by Troon Harrison
Jumanji by Chris Van Allsburg
The Magic Tree by Obinkaram T. Echewa
The Rainbabies by Laura Krauss Melmed

Picture Books for Older Readers
The King's Equal by Katherine Paterson

Easy Chapter Books
The Knight at Dawn by Mary Pope Osborne
Knights of the Kitchen Table by John Scieszka (series)

Chapter Books
The Dragonling by Jackie French Koller
Knights of the Round Table by Gwen Gross

Genre 5b. Fantasy (Talking Animals)

Picture Books
The Amazing Bone by William Steig
Doctor De Soto by William Steig
Matthew's Dream by Leo Lionni
Possum Magic by Mem Fox
Sylvester and the Magic Pebble by William Steig

Easy Chapter Books
Commander Toad in Space by Jane Yolen
My Father's Dragon by Ruth Gannett (series)

Genre 5c. Fantasy (Magical Journeys)

Picture Books
Just a Dream by Chris Van Allsburg
Little Oh by Jim LaMarche
Moon Boy by Barbara Brennor
Sector 7 by David Wisniewski (wordless)
Tuesday by David Wiesner (wordless)
Where the Wild Things Are by Maurice Sendak

Early Readers
Sir Small and the Dragonfly by Jane O'Connor

Easy Chapter Books
Dinosaurs Before Dark by Mary Pope Osborne

Chapter Books
The Dragonling by Jackie French Koller
The Farthest Away Mountain by Lynne Reid Banks
James and the Giant Peach by Roald Dahl

Genre 6. Science Fiction

[See Intermediate]

Genre 7a. Traditional Literature (African Tales)

Picture Books

Anansi Finds a Fool by Verna Aardema
Anansi the Spider: A Tale from the Ashanti by Gerald McDermott
Bimwili and the Zimwi by Verna Aardema
The Hatseller and the Monkey by Baba Wague Diakite
Imani in the Belly by Deborah M. Newton Chocolate
Who's in Rabbit's House: A Masai Tale by Verna Aardema
Why Mosquitoes Buzz in Peoples' Ears by Verna Aardema
Zomo the Rabbit: A Trickster Tale from West Africa by Gerald McDermott

Picture Books for Older Readers

The Flying Tortoise: An Igbo Tale by Tololwa M. Mollel
The Hunterman and the Crocodile by Baba Wague Diakite
Sebgugu the Glutton: A Bantu Tale from Rwanda by Verna Aardema
Traveling to Tondo: A Tale of the Nkundo of Zaire by Verna Aardema

Genre 7b. Traditional Literature (Native American Tales)

Picture Books

Arrow to the Sun by Gerald McDermott
The Boy Who Lived with Bears: And Other Iroquois Stories by Joseph Bruchac
Buffalo Dance: A Blackfoot Legend by Nancy Van Laan
Coyote by Gerald McDermott
Coyote and the Fire Stick: A Pacific Northwest Indian Tale by Barbara Diamond Goldin
Coyote Places the Stars by Harriet Peck Taylor
Crow Chief by Paul Goble
Dancing Drum: A Cherokee Legend by Terri Cohlene
Echoes of the Elders by Chief Lelooska
The First Strawberries: A Cherokee Story by Joseph Bruchac
Frog Girl by Paul Owen Lewis
The Gift of the Sacred Dog by Paul Goble
The Girl Who Loved Wild Horses by Paul Goble
How Turtle's Back Was Cracked by Gayle Ross
The Mud Pony by Caron Lee Cohen
Raven by Gerald McDermott
Sky Dogs by Jane Yolen
Supper for Crow by Pierr Morgan

Picture Books for Older Readers

Gluskabe and the Four Wishes by Joseph Bruchac
The Great Ball Game: A Muskogee Story by Joseph Bruchac
How the Stars Fell from the Sky: A Navajo Legend by Jerrie Oughton
The Legend of the Windigo: A Tale from Native North America by Gayle Ross
The Lost Children: The Boys Who Were Neglected by Paul Goble
The Magic Weaver of Rugs: A Tale of the Navajo by Jerrie Oughton
Shingebiss: An Ojibwe Legend by Nancy Van Laan
Spirit of the Cedar People by Chief Lelooska
The Story of the Milky Way: A Cherokee Tale by Joseph Bruchac and Gayle Ross

Genre 7c. Traditional Literature (Retold Tales)

Picture Books
Goldilocks and the Three Bears retold by James Marshall
Goldilocks and the Three Bears retold by Jan Brett
Hansel and Gretel retold by James Marshall
Jack and the Beanstalk retold by Steven Kellogg
Little Red Riding Hood retold by Trina Schart Hyman
Lon Po Po: A Red-Riding Hood Story from China by Ed Young
Red Riding Hood retold by James Marshall
Snow White and the Seven Dwarfs retold by Randall Jarrell
The Three Little Pigs retold by James Marshall
The Three Little Pigs retold by Steven Kellogg
The Ugly Duckling by Jerry Pinkney

Genre 7d. Traditional Literature (Tall Tales)

Picture Books
Big Jabe by Jerdine Nolen
The Bunyans by Audrey Wood
Iva Dunnit and the Big Wind by Carol Purdy
John Henry by Julius Lester
Johnny Appleseed by Steven Kellogg
Mike Fink by Steven Kellogg
Paul Bunyan by Steven Kellogg
Pecos Bill by Steven Kellogg
Sally Ann Thunder Ann Whirlwind Crockett by Steven Kellogg
Shooting Star: Annie Oakley, the Legend by Deb Dadey
Swamp Angel by Anne Isaacs

Chapter Books
Larger Than Life: The Adventures of American Legendary Heroes by Robert San Souci

Genre 7e. Traditional Literature (Fairy Tales)

Picture Books
Aladdin and the Wonderful Lamp by Carol Carrick
Bearskin by Howard Pyle
Beauty and the Beast retold by Jan Brett
Comus retold by Margaret Hodges
Dove Isabeau by Jane Yolen
The Enchanted Wood by Ruth Sanderson
Jack and the Beanstalk retold by John Howe
King Stork by Howard Pyle
The Loathsome Dragon retold by David Wiesner and Kim Kahng
Ouch! A Tale from Grimm retold by Natalie Babbitt
The Princess and the Pea retold by Janet Stevens
Princess Florecita and the Iron Shoes by John Warren Stewig
Rapunzel retold by Alix Berenzy
Saint George and the Dragon retold by Margaret Hodges
The Sleeping Beauty retold by Trina Schart Hyman
Snow White retold by Paul Heins
Snow White and the Seven Dwarfs retold by Randall Jarrell
The Sorcerer's Apprentice by Nancy Willard

Swan Lake by Margot Fonteyn
Tam Lin by Jane Yolen
The Three Princes: A Tale from the Middle East retold by Eric Kimmel
Thumbelina by Hans Christian Anderson, translated by Erik Haugaard
Tom Thumb retold by Richard Jesse Watson
The Twelve Dancing Princesses retold by Ruth Sanderson

Genre 7f. Traditional Literature (Tales of King Arthur)

Picture Books
Excalibur retold by Carol Heyer
Excalibur by Hudson Talbott
Gawain and the Green Knight by Mark Shannon
The Kitchen Knight: A Tale of King Arthur retold by Margaret Hodges
Merlin and the Dragons by Jane Yolen
Young Merlin by Robert San Souci (series)

Genre 7g. Traditional Literature (Cinderella Versions)

Picture Books
Cinderella by Charles Perrault retold by Amy Ehrlich
Cinderella by Charles Perrault retold by Diane Goode
Cinderella by David Delamare
The Egyptian Cinderella by Shirley Climo
The Korean Cinderella by Shirley Climo
Moss Gown by William Hooks
The Persian Cinderella by Shirley Climo
Princess Furball by Charlotte Huck
The Rough-Face Girl by Rafe Martin
Smoky Mountain Rose: An Appalachian Cinderella by Alan Schroeder
Sootface: An Ojibwa Cinderella Story retold by Robert San Souci
The Talking Eggs by Robert San Souci
Yeh-Shen: A Cinderella Story from China retold by Ai-Ling Louie

Picture Books for Older Readers
Cendrillon by Robert San Souci
The Golden Sandal: A Middle Eastern Cinderella Story by Rebecca Hickox
Mufaro's Beautiful Daughters: An African Tale by John Steptoe

Genre 7h. Traditional Literature (Fairy Tale Twists)

Picture Books
Ashpet: An Appalachian Tale by Joanne Compton
Bubba the Cowboy Prince: A Fractured Texas Tale by Helen Ketteman
Cindy Ellen: A Wild Western Cinderella by Susan Lowell
The Cowboy and the Black-Eyed Pea by Tony Johnston
Deep in the Forest by Brinton Turkle (wordless)
The Dragon Prince: A Chinese Beauty and the Beast Tale by Laurence Yep
Each Peach Pear Plum by Janet and Allen Ahlberg
The Emperor's Old Clothes by Kathryn Lasky
A Frog Prince by Alix Berenzy
The Frog Prince Continued by Jon Scieszka
The Giant's Toe by Brock Cole
Jim and the Beanstalk by Raymond Briggs
Little Red Riding Hood: A Newfangled Prairie Tale by Lisa Campbell Ernst

The Paper Bag Princess by Robert Munsch
Piggie Pie! by Margie Palatini
Prince Cinders by Babette Cole
Princess Smartypants by Babette Cole
The Principal's New Clothes by Stephanie Calmenson
Ruby by Michael Emberley
Somebody and the Three Blairs by Marilyn Tolhurst
Sleepless Beauty by Frances Minters
The Three Little Javelinas by Susan Lowell
The Three Little Wolves and the Big Bad Pig by Eugene Trivizas
The True Story of the 3 Little Pigs! by Jon Scieszka
Wolf! by Becky Bloom

Easy Chapter Books
Diamonds and Toads by Ellen Schecter
Sleeping Ugly by Jane Yolen

Chapter Books
The Prince of the Pond by Donna Jo Napoli

Genre 8. Nonfiction

[No Book List]

Genre 9. Poetry

Dance with Me by Barbara Juster Esbensen
Good Books, Good Times! selected by Lee Bennett Hopkins
The Great Frog Race and Other Poems by Kristine O'Connell George
Hailstones and Halibut Bones by Mary O'Neill
It's Raining Laughter by Nikki Grimes
Kinda Blue by Ann Grifalconi
Nathaniel Talking by Eloise Greenfield
Night on Neighborhood Street by Eloise Greenfield
Old Elm Speaks: Tree Poems by Kristine O'Connell George
Once Upon Ice and Other Frozen Poems by Jane Yolen
School Supplies: A Book of Poems selected by Lee Bennett Hopkins
Snow, Snow: Winter Poems for Children by Jane Yolen
Song and Dance selected by Lee Bennett Hopkins
Through Our Eyes: Poems and Pictures about Growing Up selected by Lee Bennett
   Hopkins
Water Music: Poems for Children by Jane Yolen
Weather selected by Lee Bennett Hopkins
Who Shrank My Grandmother's House? Poems of Discovery by Barbara Juster Esbensen
You and Me: Poems of Friendship selected by Salley Mavor

Time Period

[See also Intermediate]

Time Period 1. Looking into the Ancient Past
[No Book List]

Time Period 2. Middle Ages and Renaissance
[No Book List]

Time Period 3. Early Colonial
[No Book List]

Time Period 4. Revolutionary War
[No Book List]

Time Period 5. Immigration and New Beginnings
[No Book List]

Time Period 6. Westward Expansion

Picture Books
Dakota Dugout by Ann Turner
The Quilt Story by Tony Johnston
Sam Johnson and the Blue Ribbon Quilt by Lisa Campbell Ernst
Selina and the Bear Paw Quilt by Barbara Smucker
The Story of Laura Ingalls Wilder: Pioneer Girl by Megan Stine

Picture Books for Older Readers
Dandelions by Eve Bunting
If You Traveled West in a Covered Wagon by Ellen Levine
Laura Ingalls Wilder: An Author's Story by Sarah Glasscock
Trouble for Lucy by Carla Stevens
West by Covered Wagon by Dorothy Hinshaw Patent

Early Readers
Pioneer Cat by William H. Hooks

Easy Chapter Books
Chang's Paper Pony by Eleanor Coerr
The Golly Sisters Go West by Betsy Byars
The Josefina Story Quilt by Eleanor Coerr
Snowshoe Thompson by Nancy Smiler
Wagon Wheels by Barbara Brenner

Time Period 7. Slavery and the American Civil War
[No Book List]

Time Period 8. Gold Rush
[No Book List]

Time Period 9. Turn of the Century
[No Book List]

Time Period 10. Women's Rights Movement
[No Book List]

Time Period 11. Great Depression
[No Book List]

Time Period 12. World War II
[No Book List]

Time Period 13. Japanese Internment
[No Book List]

Time Period 14. Civil Rights Movement
[No Book List]

Time Period 15. Conflict in Vietnam and Southeast Asia
[No Book List]

Time Period 16. Contemporary Challenges in Other Countries
[No Book List]

Part 2

Intermediate Book Lists

See also Primary Book Lists for additional picture books and easy chapter books that would be appropriate for some intermediate grade readers. In addition, see the Upper Intermediate/Middle School Book Lists for more challenging chapter books.

Themes

[See also Primary and Upper Intermediate/Middle School]

Theme 1. Reaching Out to Others/Friendship

Picture Books for Older Readers
Be Good to Eddie Lee by Virginia Fleming
Collector of Moments by Quint Buchholz
Drylongso by Virginia Hamilton
Flags by Maxine Trottier
Josepha: A Prairie Boy's Story by Jim McGugan
Just Like New by Ainslie Manson
Nadia's Hands by Karen English
Nobiah's Well by Donna Guthrie
The Orphan Boy by Tololwa M. Mollel
Pink and Say by Patricia Polacco
Smoky Night by Eve Bunting
Tomás and the Library Lady by Pat Mora

Chapter Books
Absolutely Normal Chaos by Sharon Creech
Anastasia Krupnik by Lois Lowry (series)
Babe: The Gallant Pig by Dick King-Smith
Bandit's Moon by Paul Fleischman
Because of Winn-Dixie by Kate DiCamillo
The Best School Year Ever by Barbara Robinson
The BFG by Roald Dahl
Bingo Brown and the Language of Love by Betsy Byars
The Boys Start the War by Phyllis Reynolds Naylor
Building a Bridge by Lisa Shook Begaye
Daphne's Book by Mary Downing Hahn
Don't Call Me Beanhead by Susan Wojchiechowski
Finding Buck McHenry by Alfred Slote
The Flip-flop Girl by Katherine Paterson
Freckle Juice by Judy Blume
The Girls Get Even by Phyllis Reynolds Naylor
Henry and Ribsy by Beverly Cleary
Loudmouth George by Nancy Carlson

Next-Door Neighbors by Sarah Ellis
The Pennywhistle Tree by Doris Buchanan Smith
The Pinballs by Betsy Byars
Ramona Quimby, Age 8 by Beverly Cleary (series)
Runaway Home by Patricia McKissack
The Secret Life of Amanda K. Woods by Ann Cameron
Solo Girl by Andrea Davis Pinkney
Tales of a Fourth Grade Nothing by Judy Blume
Thank You, Jackie Robinson by Barbara Cohen
To JayKae: Life Stinks by Jean Davies Okimoto
What's a Daring Detective Like Me Doing in the Doghouse? by Linda Bailey

Theme 2. Family Issues

Picture Books for Older Readers
The Bat Boy and His Violin by Gavin Curtis
Dandelions by Eve Bunting
Ma Dear's Aprons by Patricia McKissack
My Ol' Man by Patricia Polacco
My Rotten Redheaded Brother by Patricia Polacco
Stringbean's Trip to the Shining Sea by Vera and Jennifer Williams
The Table Where Rich People Sit by Byrd Baylor
Tea with Milk by Allen Say
What You Know First by Patricia MacLachlan
Working Cotton by Sherley Anne Williams
Your Move by Eve Bunting

Easy Chapter Books
Mister and Me by Kimberly Willis Holt
Not My Dog by Colby Rodowsky

Chapter Books
All About Sam by Lois Lowry
Arthur, For the Very First Time by Patricia MacLachlan
Autumn Street by Lois Lowry
Black-Eyed Susan by Jennifer Armstrong
The Boxcar Children by Gertrude Chandler Warner (series)
Cassie Binegar by Patricia MacLachlan
Crossing the Starlight Bridge by Alice Mead
Discovering One Thing I'm Good At by Karen Lynn Williams
Fig Pudding by Ralph Fletcher
The Hideout by Eve Bunting
The In-Between Days by Eve Bunting
It's Like This, Cat by Emily Neville
Jim Ugly by Sid Fleischman
Just Juice by Karen Hesse
Justin and the Best Biscuits in the World by Walter and Mildred Pitts
Lavender by Karen Hesse
Little House on the Prairie by Laura Ingalls Wilder (series)
Maybe Yes, Maybe No, Maybe Maybe by Susan Patron
Radiance Descending by Paula Fox
Ramona's World by Beverly Cleary (series)
Regular Guy by Sarah Weeks

Sarah, Plain and Tall by Patricia MacLachlan
Skylark by Patricia MacLachlan
Socks by Beverly Cleary
Superfudge by Judy Blume
The Trading Game by Alfred Slote
The War with Grandpa by Robert Kimmel Smith
Yang the Third and Her Impossible Family by Lensey Namioka (series)
The Zebra Wall by Kevin Henkes

Theme 3. Generations Learning from One Another

Picture Books for Older Readers

The Day GoGo Went to Vote by Elinor Betezat Sisulu
Grandfather's Journey by Allen Say
How Does it Feel to Grow Old? by Norma Farber
The Hundred Penny Box by Sharon Bell Mathis
The Keeping Quilt by Patricia Polacco
Lucy's Picture by Nicola Moon
Luka's Quilt by Georgia Guback
The Memory Box by Mary Bahr
Momma, Where Are You From? by Marie Bradby
Muskrat Will Be Swimming by Cheryl Savageau
My Great-Aunt Arizona by Gloria Houston
The Night the Grandfathers Danced by Linda Theresa Raczek
The Patchwork Quilt by Valerie Flournoy
The Remembering Box by Eth Clifford
Something Special by Vera B. Williams
Storm in the Night by Mary Stolz
The Summer My Father Was Ten by Pat Brisson
Sunshine Home by Eve Bunting
Tales of a Gambling Grandma by Dayal Kaur Khalsa
Three Cheers for Catherine the Great! by Cari Best
The Two of Them by Aliki
The Unbreakable Code by Sarah Hoagland Hunter
A Walk to the Great Mystery by Virginia Stroud
The Wall by Eve Bunting
Wednesday Surprise by Eve Bunting
Where is Grandpa? by T. A. Barron
The Year of Fire by Teddy Jam

Chapter Books

Blackberries in the Dark by Mavis Jukes
An Early Winter by Marion Dane Bauer
Finding Buck McHenry by Alfred Slote
The Last Lobo by Roland Smith
Leaving Emma by Nancy Steele Brokaw
My Daniel by Pam Conrad
The Snoop by Jane Resh Thomas
Sun and Spoon by Kevin Henkes
Take a Chance, Gramps by Jean Davies Okimoto
The Trolls by Polly Horvath
The War with Grandpa by Robert Kimmel Smith

Theme 4a. Challenges (Pursuing a Dream)

Picture Books for Older Readers
A Band of Angels by Deborah Hopkinson
Bill Pickett: Rodeo-Ridin' Cowboy by Andrea Davis Pinkney
The Day GoGo Went to Vote by Elinor Betezat Sisulu
El Chino by Allen Say
How Many Days to America? by Eve Bunting
If I Only Had a Horn: Young Louis Armstrong by Roxanne Orgill
Jingle Dancer by Cynthia Leitich Smith
My Dream of Martin Luther King by Faith Ringgold
My Rows and Piles of Coins by Tololwa M. Mollel
Richard Wright and the Library Card by William Miller
Uncle Jed's Barbershop by Margaree King Mitchell

Easy Chapter Books
The Skates of Uncle Richard by Carol Fenner

Theme 4b. Challenges (Taking Action to Care for Others)

Picture Books for Older Readers
Birdie's Lighthouse by Deborah Hopkinson
Garbage Creek and Other Stories by W. D. Valgardson

Chapter Books
Toughboy and Sister by Kirkpatrick Hill
Winter Camp by Kirkpatrick Hill

Theme 4c. Challenges (Persevering Despite Obstacles)

Picture Books for Older Readers
The Babe and I by David Adler
Baseball Saved Us by Ken Mochizuki
Birdie's Lighthouse by Deborah Hopkinson
Black Whiteness: Admiral Byrd Alone in the Antarctic by Robert Burleigh
Blue Jay in the Desert by Marlene Shigekawa
The Bracelet by Yoshiko Uchida
Fly Away Home by Eve Bunting
Home to Medicine Mountain by Chiori Santiago
I Have Heard of a Land by Joyce Carol Thomas
Cassie's Journey by Brett Harvey
Ghost Train by Paul Yee
Lights on the River by Jane Resh Thomas
The Lotus Seed by Sherry Garland
The Memory Coat by Elvira Woodruff
Teammates by Peter Golenbock
Through My Eyes by Ruby Bridges
A Train to Somewhere by Eve Bunting
When Jessie Came Across the Sea by Amy Hest
Zora Hurston and the Chinaberry Tree by William Miller

Easy Chapter Books
Mieko and the Fifth Treasure by Eleanor Coerr

Chapter Books
Daughter of Suqua by Diane Johnston Hamm
Under the Hawthorne Tree by Marta Conlon-McKenna

Theme 4d. Challenges (Challenges of Growing Up)

Picture Books
Chrysanthemum by Kevin Henkes
Lilly's Purple Plastic Purse by Kevin Henkes
Ruby the Copycat by Peggy Rathmann

Picture Books for Older Readers
Too Many Tamales by Gary Soto
The Very Last First Time by Jan Andrews
When Jo Louis Won the Title by Belinda Rochelle

Easy Chapter Book
Pia Lia's First Day by Michelle Edwards

Chapter Books
Are You There, God? It's Me, Margaret by Judy Blume
Cassandra—Live at Carnegie Hall by Nancy Hopper
Darnell Rock Reporting by Walter Dean Myers
Dear Mr. Henshaw by Beverly Cleary
Ever-Clever Elisa by Johanna Hurwitz
The Flunking of Joshua T. Bates by Susan Shreve
In the Year of the Boar and Jackie Robinson by Bette Bao Lord
Jack on the Tracks: Four Seasons of Fifth Grade by Jack Gantos
James and the Giant Peach by Roald Dahl
Judy Moody was in a Mood. Not a Good Mood. A Bad Mood. by Megan McDonald
Keep Ms. Sugarman in the Fourth Grade by Elizabeth Levy
Spider Boy by Ralph Fletcher
Tales of a Fourth Grade Nothing by Judy Blume
Thank You, Dr. Martin Luther King, Jr.! by Eleanora Tate
There's a Boy in the Girls' Bathroom by Louis Sachar
Trumpet of the Swan by E. B. White
You're a Brave Man, Julius Zimmerman by Claudia Mills

Theme 4e. Challenges (Overcoming Personal Challenges)

Picture Books for Older Readers
Danny and the Kings by Susan Cooper
Listen for the Bus: David's Story by Patricia McMahon
Sadako by Eleanor Coerr
Thank You, Mr. Falker by Patricia Polacco
Tight Times by Barbara Shook Hazen

Easy Chapter Book
Sadako and the Thousand Paper Cranes by Eleanor Coerr

Chapter Books
Do You Remember the Color Blue? by Sally Hobart Alexander
The Fear Place by Phyllis Reynolds Naylor

Just Call Me Stupid by Tom Birdseye
Just Juice by Karen Hesse
Kelly's Creek by Doris Buchanan Smith
On My Honor by Marion Dane Bauer
A Taste of Blackberries by Mavis Jukes

Theme 4f. Challenges (Finding a Place to Belong)

Picture Books for Older Readers
Bonesy and Isabel by Michael Rosen
The Boy Who Wanted a Family by Shirley Gordon
Onion Tears by Diana Kidd
Radio Man by Arthur Dorros
Strong to the Hoop by John Coy

Chapter Books
Eagle Song by Joseph Bruchac
The Gadget War by Betsy Duffey
The Kid in the Red Jacket by Barbara Park
Shoeshine Girl by Clyde Robert Bulla
There's a Boy in the Girls' Bathroom by Louis Sachar

Theme 5. Courage

Picture Books for Older Readers
Aunt Harriet's Underground Railroad in the Sky by Faith Ringgold
The Boy Called Slow by Joseph Bruchac
Brave as a Mountain Lion by Ann Herbert Scott
Fa Mulan: The Story of a Woman Warrior by Robert San Souci
Fire on the Mountain by Jane Kurtz
Gift Horse: A Lakota Story by S. D. Nelson
Katie's Trunk by Ann Turner
The Lily Cupboard by Shulamith Levey Oppenheim
Mirette on the High Wire by Emily Arnold McCully
A Promise is a Promise by Robert Munsch, Michael Kusugak, and Vladanya Krykorka
The Story of Ruby Bridges by Robert Coles
The Streets of Gold by Rosemary Wells
Sweet Clara and the Freedom Quilt by Deborah Hopkinson
Tales from Gold Mountain by Paul Yee
Wilma Unlimited by Kathleen Krull

Easy Chapter Book
Stone Fox by John Reynolds Gardiner

Chapter Books
Hatchet by Gary Paulsen
Mrs. Frisby and the Rats of NIMH by Robert C. O'Brien
Night of the Twisters by Ivy Ruckman
Nory Ryan's Song by Patricia Reilly Giff
Rescue Josh McGuire by Ben Mikaelsen
The River by Gary Paulsen
Sasquatch by Roland Smith
Sparrowhawk Red by Ben Mikaelsen
Star in the Storm by Joann Hiatt Harlow
Totally Disgusting by Bill Wallace

Theme 6. Standing Up for Your Beliefs

Picture Book
Aani and the Tree Huggers by Jeannine Atkins

Picture Books for Older Readers
The Ballot Box Battle by Emily Arnold McCully
The Bobbin Girl by Emily Arnold McCully
A Boy Becomes a Man at Wounded Knee by Ted Wood
Crazy Horse's Vision by Joseph Bruchac
Dear Benjamin Banneker by Andrea Davis Pinkney
The Death of the Iron Horse by Paul Goble
Friends from the Other Side by Gloria Anzaldua
Ghandi by Leonard Everett Fisher
Ghost Dance by Alice McLerran
Granddaddy's Gift by Margaree King Mitchell
Harriet and the Promised Land by Jacob Lawrence
If a Bus Could Talk by Faith Ringgold
Joan of Arc by Diane Stanley
Leagues Apart: The Men and Times of the Negro Baseball Leagues by Lawrence Ritter
Mandela by Floyd Cooper
Minty: A Story of Young Harriet Tubman by Alan Schroeder
Molly Bannaky by Alice McGill
My Dream of Martin Luther King by Faith Ringgold
Now Let Me Fly: The Story of a Slave Family by Dolores Johnson
Passage to Freedom: The Sugihara Story by Ken Mochizuki
The People Who Hugged Trees by Deborah Lee Rose
She's Wearing a Dead Bird on Her Head by Kathryn Lasky
Sister Anne's Hands by Maribeth Lorbiecki
Starry Messenger by Peter Sis
Teammates by Peter Golenbock

Easy Chapter Book
Eleanor Everywhere by Monica Kulling

Chapter Books
Edwina Victorious by Susan Bonners
Frindle by Andrew Clements
Harriet Beecher Stowe and the Beecher Preachers by Jean Fritz
Just a Few Words, Mr. Lincoln: The Story of the Gettysburg Address by Jean Fritz
The Landry News by Andrew Clements
Rosa Parks: My Story by Rosa Parks with Jim Haskins
What Are You Figuring Now, Benjamin Banneker? by Jeri Ferris
You Want Women to Vote, Lizzie Stanton? by Jean Fritz

Theme 7. Justice

[See Upper Intermediate/Middle School]

Theme 8. Survival

[See Upper Intermediate/Middle School]

Theme 9. Respecting Nature

Picture Books for Older Readers
Henry Hikes to Fitchburg by Donald B. Johnson

Moonstick: The Seasons of the Sioux by Eve Bunting
Prince William by Gloria Rand
A River Ran Wild by Lynne Cherry
The Shaman's Apprentice: A Tale of the Amazon Rain Forest by Lynne Cherry and
    Mark Plotkin
Snowflake Bentley by Jacqueline Briggs Martin
Volcano: The Eruption and Healing of Mount St. Helens by Patricia Lauber
Where Once There Was a Wood by Denise Fleming

Easy Chapter Books
Hill of Fire by Thomas Lewis

Chapter Books
One Day in the Tropical Rainforest by Jean Craighead George
The Talking Earth by Jean Craighead George
Tornado by Betsy Byars
Who Really Killed Cock Robin? An Ecological Mystery by Jean Craighead George

Theme 10. Caring for Animals

Picture Books for Older Readers
The Clay Ladies by Michael Bedard
Come Back, Salmon by Molly Cone

Early Readers
Sam and the Sea Cow by Francine Jacobs

Easy Chapter Books
The Amazing Panda Adventure by John Wilcox and Steven Allredge
Andy Bear: A Polar Cub Grows Up at the Zoo by Ginny Johnston and Judy Cutchins
Buddy, the First Seeing Eye Dog by Eva Moore
Dancing with Manatees by Faith McNulty
Dolphin's First Day: The Story of a Bottlenose Dolphin by Kathleen Weidner Zoehfeld
Ibis: A True Whale Story by John Himmelman
Not My Dog by Colby Rodowsky
Outside Dog by Charlotte Pomerantz
Sable by Karen Hesse
Stone Fox by John Reynolds Gardiner
The True Story of Balto: The Bravest Dog Ever by Natalie Standiford
The True Story of Corky, the Blind Seal by Georgeanne Irvine

Chapter Books
Because of Winn-Dixie by Kate DiCamillo
Bill by Chap Reaver
Cages by Peg Kehret
The Comeback Dog by Jane Resh Thomas
Frightful's Mountain by Jean Craighead George
Harry's Mad by Dick King-Smith
The Incredible Journey by Sheila Burnford
Midnight Fox by Betsy Byars
Old Yeller by Fred Gipson
The One-Eyed Cat by Paula Fox
On the Far Side of the Mountain by Jean Craighead George
Protecting Marie by Kevin Henkes
Rascal by Sterling North

Shiloh by Phyllis Reynolds Naylor (series)
Sounder by William Armstrong
Star in the Storm by Joan Hiatt Harlow
The Tarantula in My Purse and 172 Other Wild Pets by Jean Craighead George
There's an Owl in My Shower by Jean Craighead George
The Trouble with Tuck by Theodore Taylor
Where the Red Fern Grows by Wilson Rawls

Genres

[See also Primary and Upper Intermediate/Middle School]

Genre 1. Fiction

[No Book List]

Genre 2. Historical Fiction

[See Time Periods]

Genre 3a. Biography (Sports Heroes)

Picture Books
Satchel Paige by Lesa Cline-Ransome

Picture Books for Older Readers
America's Champion Swimmer: Gertrude Ederle by David Adler
Dirt on Their Skirts: The Story of the Young Women Who Won the World Championship by Doreen Rappaport and Lyndall Callan
Leagues Apart: The Men and Times of the Negro Baseball Leagues by Lawrence S. Ritter
Lou Gehrig: The Luckiest Man by David Adler
Teammates by Peter Golenbock
Wilma Unlimited by Kathleen Krull

Chapter Books
Black Diamond: The Story of Negro Baseball by Patricia McKissack and Frederick L. McKissack
Jim Abbot: Against All Odds by Ellen Emerson White
Stealing Home: The Story of Jackie Robinson by Barry Denenberg
The Story of Jackie Robinson: Bravest Man in Baseball by Margaret Davidson

Genre 3b. Biography (Imagining the Future: Aviators, Explorers, Inventors and Scientists)

Picture Books
The Glorious Flight by Alice Provensen and Martin Provensen
Nobody Owns the Sky by Reeve Lindbergh

Picture Books for Older Readers
Always Inventing: A Photobiography of Alexander Graham Bell by Tom L. Matthews
Black Whiteness: Admiral Byrd Alone in the Antarctic by Robert Burleigh
Sky Pioneer by Corinne Szabo

Easy Chapter Books
Amelia Earhart: Pioneer of the Sky by John Parlin
Five Brave Explorers by Wade Hudson
Five Brave Inventors by Wade Hudson

Chapter Books

An American Hero: The Story of Charles Lindbergh by Berry Deneberg

Elizabeth Blackwell: A Doctor's Triumph by Nancy Kline

Going Solo by Roald Dahl

Girls Think of Everything: Stories of Ingenious Inventions by Women by Catherine Thimmesh

Henry Ford: Young Man with Ideas by Hazel Aird

Mae Jemison: Space Scientist by Gail Sakurai

Outward Dreams: Black Inventors and Their Inventions by Jim Haskins

Rachel Carson: Pioneer of Ecology by Kathleen Kudlinski

Sally Ride: Shooting for the Stars by Jane Hurwitz and Sue Hurwitz

The Story of George Washington Carver by Eva Moore

Wilbur and Orville Wright: The Flight to Adventure by Louis Saban

The Wright Brothers at Kitty Hawk by Donald Sobol

Genre 3c. Biography (Freedom Fighters)

Picture Books for Older Readers

Minty: A Story of Young Harriet Tubman by Alan Schroeder

Passage to Freedom: The Sugihara Story by Ken Mochizuki

Easy Chapter Books

Eleanor Everywhere: The Life of Eleanor Roosevelt by Monica Kulling

Chapter Books

Eleanor Roosevelt: Fighter for Social Justice by Ann Weil

Freedom Train: The Story of Harriet Tubman by Dororthy Sterling

Harriet Beecher Stowe and the Beecher Preachers by Jean Fritz

I Have a Dream: The Story of Martin Luther King by Margaret Davidson

The Story of Harriet Tubman: Conductor of the Underground Railroad by Kate McMullan

Two Tickets to Freedom: The True Story of William and Ellen Craft, Fugitive Slaves by Florence Freedman

Genre 3d. Biography (Facing Challenges)

Picture Books for Older Readers

Bill Pickett: Rodeo Ridin' Cowboy by Andrea Davis Pinkney

Last Princess: The Story of Princess Kai'iulani of Hawaii by Fay Stanley

Vision of Beauty: The Story of Sarah Breedlove Walker by Kathryn Lasky

Chapter Books

Helen Keller by Margaret Davidson

Helen Keller: From Tragedy to Triumph by Katherine E. Wilkie

Helen Keller's Teacher by Margaret Davidson

In the Line of Fire: Eight Women War Spies by George Sullivan

Louis Braille: The Boy Who Invented Books for the Blind by Margaret Davidson

New Kids in Town: Oral Histories of Immigrant Teens by Janet Bode

Out of Darkness: The Story of Louis Braille by Russell Freedman

They Led the Way: 14 American Women by Johanna Johnston

Genre 3e. Biography (Artists, Dancers, Writers, and Musicians)

Picture Books

Alvin Ailey by Andrea Davis Pinkney

Charlie Parker Played Be Bop by Chris Raschka

Picture Books for Older Readers
Bard of Avon: The Story of William Shakespeare by Diane Stanley and Peter Vennema
Coming Home: From the Life of Langston Hughes by Quint Buchholz
Duke Ellington: The Piano Prince and his Orchestra by Andrea Davis Pinkney
If I Only Had a Horn: Young Louis Armstrong by Roxanne Orgill
Mysterious Thelonious by Chris Raschka
Satchmo's Blues by Alan Schroeder

Genre 4. Mystery

Picture Books for Older Readers
The Mary Celeste: An Unsolved Mystery from History by Jane Yolen and Heidi Elisabet Yolen Stemple

Chapter Books
The Clearing by Dorothy Reynolds Miller
The Curse of the Blue Figurine by John Bellairs
Danger in Quicksand Swamp by Bill Wallace
Dead Man in Indian Creek by Mary Downing Hahn
The Egypt Game by Zilpha Keatley Snyder
The Hideout by Eve Bunting
The House with a Clock in Its Walls by John Bellairs
Is Anybody There? by Eve Bunting
Magic of the Black Mirror by Ruth Chew
The Man Who Was Poe by Avi
Night Cry by Phyllis Reynolds Naylor
Something Upstairs by Avi
Terror at the Zoo by Peg Kehret
The View from the Cherry Tree by Willo Davis Roberts
The Westing Game by Ellen Raskin
Windcatcher by Avi

Genre 5a. Fantasy

Picture Books for Older Readers
The Tale I Told Sasha by Nancy Willard

Easy Chapter Books
Fantastic Mr. Fox by Roald Dahl
The Time Warp Trio by Jon Scieszka (series)

Chapter Books
The BFG by Roald Dahl
A Brush with Magic by William Brooke
The Castle in the Attic by Elizabeth Winthrop (series)
Charlie and the Chocolate Factory by Roald Dahl
The Dragon's Boy by Jane Yolen
The Fairy Rebel by Lynne Reid Banks
The Forest by Janet Lisle
George's Marvelous Medicine by Roald Dahl
James and the Giant Peach by Roald Dahl
A Glory of Unicorns edited by Bruce Coville
Jeremy Thatcher, Dragon Hatcher by Bruce Coville
Matilda by Roald Dahl
Song of the Wanderer by Bruce Coville

Time Cat by Lloyd Alexander
Totally Disgusting by Bill Wallace
The Twits by Roald Dahl
Wizard's Hall by Jane Yolen
The Wizard's Map by Jane Yolen (series)

Genre 5b. Fantasy (Talking Animals)

Chapter Books
Babe the Gallant Pig by Howe Dick King-Smith
Bunnicula by Deborah and James Howe (series)
Charlotte's Web by E. B. White
Cricket in Times Square by George Selden
Fantastic Mr. Fox by Roald Dahl
The Mouse and the Motorcycle by Beverly Cleary
Mr. Popper's Penguins by Richard and Florence Atwater
Poppy by Avi
Poppy and Rye by Avi
Stuart Little by E. B. White
Three Terrible Trins by Dick King-Smith

Genre 5c. Fantasy (Ghost Stories)

Chapter Books
Pleasing the Ghost by Sharon Creech
School Spirits by Michael Tunnell
Time for Andrew by Mary Downing Hahn
Wait Till Helen Comes by Mary Downing Hahn

Genre 6. Science Fiction

[See Upper Intermediate/Middle School]

Genre 7. Traditional Literature

[See also Primary]

Picture Books
Borreguita and the Coyote: A Tale from Ayutla, Mexico by Verna Aardema
The Dragon Prince: A Chinese Beauty and the Beast Tale by Laurence Yep
The Eye of the Needle by Teri Sloat
Papagayo: The Mischief Maker by Gerald McDermott
The People of Corn: A Mayan Story by Mary-Joan Gerson
Rockabye Crocodile by Jose Aruego and Ariane Dewey

Picture Books for Older Readers
Fa Mulan: The Story of a Woman Warrior by Robert San Souci
Golem by David Wisniewski
Wave of the Sea-Wolf by David Wisniewski

Chapter Books
Cut from the Same Cloth: American Women of Myth, Legend, and Tall Tale by Robert San Souci
Misoso: Once Upon a Time Tales from Africa by Verna Aardema
Not One Damsel in Distress: World Folktales for Strong Girls collected by Jane Yolen
The People Could Fly by Virginia Hamilton, YA

Genre 8. Nonfiction

[No Book List]

Genre 9. Poetry

Baseball, Snakes, and Summer Squash: Poems about Growing Up by Donald Graves
Been to Yesterdays: Poems of a Life by Lee Bennett Hopkins
Brown Angels: An Album of Pictures and Verse by Walter Dean Myers
Brown Honey in Broomwheat Tea by Joyce Carol Thomas
The Dragons Are Singing Tonight by Jack Prelutsky
The Earth Under Sky Bear's Feet: Native American Poems of the Land by Joseph Bruchac
Extra Innings: Baseball Poems selected by Lee Bennett Hopkins
If I Were in Charge of the World and Other Worries by Judith Viorst
Inner Chimes: Poems on Poetry selected by Bobbye Goldstein
A Jar of Tiny Stars: Poems by NCTE Award-Winning Poets edited by Bernice Cullinan
Joyful Noise: Poems for Two Voices by Paul Fleischman
Love Letters by Arnold Adoff
Meet Danitra Brown by Nikki Grimes
Navajo: Visions and Voices Across the Mesa by Shonto Begay
Pass It On: African American Poetry for Children selected by Wade Hudson
Ten-Second Rainshowers: Poems by Young People selected by Sandford Lyne
Thirteen Moons on Turtle's Back: A Native American Year of Moons by Joseph Bruchac and Jonathan London
This Big Sky by Pat Mora
Winter Poems selected by Barbara Rogasky

Time Periods

[See also Primary and Upper Intermediate/Middle School]

Time Period 1. Looking into the Ancient Past

[See Upper Intermediate/Middle School]

Time Period 2. Middle Ages and Renaissance

[See Upper Intermediate/Middle School]

Time Period 3a. Early Colonial

Picture Books for Older Readers
Dear Benjamin Banneker by Andrea Davis Pinkney
Maria's Comet by Deborah Hopkinson
Molly Bannaky by Alice McGill
Samuel Eaton's Day by Kate Waters

Chapter Books
Pirate's Promise by Clyde Robert Bulla

Time Period 3b. Early Colonial (Relationships between Colonists and Native Americans)

Chapter Books
Between Two Worlds by Candice Ransome
Calico Captive by Elizabeth George Speare

The Double Life of Pocohontas by Jean Fritz
Guests by Michael Dorris
I Am Regina by Sally Keehn
Indian Captive by Lois Lenski
Morning Girl by Michael Dorris
Sign of the Beaver by Elizabeth George Speare
Trouble's Daughter by Katherine Kirkpatrick

Time Period 4. Revolutionary War

Picture Books for Older Readers
Katie's Trunk by Ann Turner
Redcoats and Petticoats by Katherine Kirkpatrick

Chapter Books
The Arrow over the Door by Joseph Bruchac
Buttons for General Washington by Peter Roop and Connie Roop
The Fighting Ground by Avi
George Washington's Socks by Elvira Woodruff
The Hollow Tree by Janet Lunn
My Brother Sam is Dead by James Lincoln Collier and Christopher Collier
The Poison Place by Mary Lyons
Sarah Bishop by Scott O'Dell
War Comes to Willy Freeman by James Lincoln Collier and Christopher Collier
Who Comes with Cannons? by Patricia Beatty

Time Period 5. Immigration and New Beginnings

Picture Books
Pepe the Lamplighter by Elisa Bartone

Picture Books for Older Readers
Ghost Train by Paul Yee
Grandfather's Journey by Allan Say
How Many Days to America? by Eve Bunting
Journey to Ellis Island by Carol Bierman
The Keeping Quilt by Patricia Polacco
The Memory Coat by Elvira Woodruff
The Streets of Gold by Rosemary Wells
When Jessie Came Across the Sea by Amy Hest

Early Reader
The Long Way to a New Land by Joan Sandin

Easy Chapter Book
Molly's Pilgrim by Barbara Cohen

Chapter Books
Call Me Ruth by Marilyn Sachs
Immigrant Kids by Russell Freedman
Land of Hope by Joan Lowery Nixon (series)
Letters from Rifka by Karen Hesse
A Long Way to a New Land by Joan Sandin
The Orphan of Ellis Island by Elvira Woodruff
A Place Not Home by Eva Wiseman

Shannon by Kathleen Kudlinski (series)
Where Did Your Family Come From? by Melvin and Gilda Berger

Time Period 6. Westward Expansion (Multiple Perspectives)

Picture Books for Older Readers

Black Cowboys, Wild Horses: A True Story by Julius Lester
A Boy Called Slow by Joseph Bruchac
Cassie's Journey by Brett Harvey
Cheyenne Again by Eve Bunting
Crazy Horse's Vision by Joseph Bruchac
Daily Life in a Covered Wagon by Paul Erickson
Dandelions by Eve Bunting
Ghost Dance by Alice McLerran
Gift Horse by S. D. Nelson
Josepha: A Prairie Boy's Story by Jim McGugan
Laura's Album by William Anderson
My Prairie Year by Brett Harvey
Orphan Train Rider by Andrea Warren
Rachel's Journal by Marissa Moss
Train to Somewhere by Eve Bunting
West by Covered Wagon by Dorothy Hinshaw Patent

Chapter Books

Adaline Falling Star by Mary Pope Osborne
The Birchbark House by Louise Erdrich
Black-Eyed Susan by Jennifer Armstrong
Bound for Oregon by Jean Van Leeuwen
The Cabin Faced West by Jean Fritz
Caddie Woodlawn by Carol Ryrie Brink
Calico Bush by Rachael Field
The Captain's Dog by Roland Smith
Daughter of Suqua by Diane Johnston Hamm
Fortune's Journey by Bruce Coville
The Gentleman Outlaw and Me—Eli by Mary Downing Hahn
Jericho's Journey by G. Clifton Wisler
The Journey Home by Isabelle Holland
The Legend of Jimmy Spoon by Kristiana Gregory
The Life and Death of Crazy Horse by Russell Freedman
Little Farm in the Ozarks by Roger Lea McBride
Little House on the Prairie by Laura Ingalls Wilder (series)
My Daniel by Pam Conrad
Prairie Song by Pam Conrad
Sarah, Plain and Tall by Patricia MacLaughlin
Save Queen of Sheba by Louise Moeri
Sing Down the Moon by Scott O'Dell
Shooting Star by Sheila Solomon Klass
Skylark by Patricia MacLaughlin
The Story of Laura Ingalls Wilder, Pioneer Girl by Megan Stine
Stream to the River, River to the Sea by Scott O'Dell
Thunder Rolling in the Mountains by Scott O'Dell and Elizabeth Hall

Ticket to Curlew by Celia Barker Lottridge
Weasel by Cynthia DeFelice
Wings to Fly by Celia Barker Lottridge

Time Period 7. Slavery and the American Civil War

Picture Books
Cecil's Story by George Ella Lyon
Follow the Drinking Gourd by Jeanette Winter

Picture Books for Older Readers
Aunt Harriet's Underground Railroad in the Sky by Faith Ringgold
Civil War Artist by Taylor Morrison
Harriet and the Promised Land by Jacob Lawrence
In the Time of the Drums by Kim L. Siegelson
Minty: A Story of Young Harriet Tubman by Alan Schroeder
More Than Anything Else by Marie Bradby
Now Let Me Fly by Delores Johnson
Nettie's Trip South by Ann Turner
Pink and Say by Patricia Polacco
Sweet Clara and the Freedom Quilt by Deborah Hopkinson
The Wagon by Tony Johnston

Easy Chapter Books
The Drinking Gourd by Ferdinand Maijo
Thunder at Gettysburg by Patricia Lee Gauch

Chapter Books
Across Five Aprils by Irene Hunt
Anthony Burns: The Defeat and Triumph of a Fugitive Slave by Virginia Hamilton
Brady by Jean Fritz
Bright Freedom's Song by Gloria Houston
Bull Run by Paul Fleishman
Changes for Addie by Connie Parker (series)
Charlie Skedaddle by Patricia Beatty
A Dangerous Promise by Joan Lowery Nixon (series)
The Drummer Boy of Vicksburg by G. Clifton Wisler
Forty Acres and Maybe a Mule by Harriette Gillem Robinet
Gentle Annie by Mary Francis Shura
A Girl Called Boy by Belinda Hermence
Harriet Beecher Stowe and the Beecher Preachers by Jean Fritz
I Thought My Soul Would Rise and Fly: The Diary of Patsy, a Freed Girl by Joyce Hansen
Jayhawker by Patricia Beatty
Just a Few Words, Mr. Lincoln by Jean Fritz
Mr. Lincoln's Drummer by G. Clifton Wisler
No Man's Land: A Young Soldier's Story by Susan Campbell Bartoletti
Out from this Place by Joyce Hansen
Red Cap by G. Clifton Wisler
Shades of Gray by Carolyn Reeder
Steal Away by Jennifer Armstrong
Stealing Freedom by Elisa Lynn Carbone
Turn Homeward, Hannalee by Patricia Beatty
"Wanted Dead or Alive": The True Story of Harriet Tubman by A. McGovern

Which Way Freedom? by Joyce Hansen
Who Is Carrie? by James Lincoln Collier and Christopher Collier

Time Period 8. Gold Rush
[See Upper Intermediate/Middle School]

Time Period 9. Turn of the Century

Picture Books
Mailing May by Michael O. Tunnell
Marven of the Great North Woods by Kathryn Lasky

Picture Books for Older Readers
Coming Home: From the Life of Langston Hughes by Floyd Cooper
The Glorious Flight by Alice Provensen and Martin Provensen
The Great Migration: An American Story by Jacob Lawrence
Mirette on the High Wire by Emily Arnold McCully
True Heart by Marissa Moss

Easy Chapter Book
Fire at the Triangle Factory by Holly Littlefield

Chapter Books
Earthquake! A Story of Old San Francisco by Kathleen Kudlinski
Earthquake at Dawn by Kristiana Gregory
Growing Up in Coal Country by Susan Campbell Bartoletti
Home Child by Barbara Haworth-Attard
I Am Lavina Cumming by Susan Lowell
Preacher's Boy by Katherine Paterson
Promise Song by Linda Holeman
S.O.S. Titanic by Eve Bunting
Star in the Storm by Joan Hiatt Harlow
Starfisher by Laurence Yep

Time Period 10. Women's Rights Movement
[See Upper Intermediate/Middle School]

Time Period 11. Great Depression

Picture Books for Older Readers
The Babe and I by David Adler
The Dust Bowl by David Booth
The Gardener by Sarah Stewart
Home to Medicine Mountain by Chiori Santiago
Uncle Jed's Barbershop by Margaree King Mitchell

Easy Chapter Book
Dust for Dinner by Ann Turner

Chapter Books
Breakaway by Paul Yee
The Friendship by Mildred Taylor
Jar of Dreams by Yoshiko Uchida
Let the Circle Be Unbroken by Mildred Taylor
Mississippi Bridge by Mildred Taylor
Oh Those Harper Girls by Kathleen Karr

Potato: A Tale of the Great Depression by Kate Lied
Purely Rosie Pearl by Patricia Cochrane

Time Period 12. World War II

[See Upper Intermediate/Middle School]

Time Period 13. Japanese Internment

[See Upper Intermediate/Middle School]

Time Period 14. Civil Rights Movement

Picture Books for Older Readers

Granddaddy's Gift by Margaree King Mitchell
If a Bus Could Talk by Faith Ringgold
My Dream of Martin Luther King, Jr. by Faith Ringgold
National Civil Rights Museum Celebrates Everyday People by Alice Faye Dunkin
The Story of Ruby Bridges by Robert Coles
Teammates by Peter Golenbock
Through My Eyes by Ruby Bridges
White Socks Only by Evelyn Coleman

Easy Chapter Book

Mississippi Bridge by Mildred Taylor

Chapter Books

The Gold Cadillac by Mildred Taylor
Rosa Parks: My Story by Rosa Parks and Jim Haskins

Time Period 15. Conflict in Vietnam and Southeast Asia

[See Upper Intermediate/Middle School]

Time Period 16. Contemporary Challenges in Other Countries (South Africa)

[See Upper Intermediate/Middle School]

Part 3

Upper Intermediate/Middle School Book Lists

See also the Intermediate Book Lists for less challenging chapter books that would be appropriate for some upper intermediate grade and middle school readers.

Themes

[See also Intermediate]

Theme 1. Reaching Out to Others/Friendship

Picture Books for Older Readers
Be Good to Eddie Lee by Virginia Fleming
Bonesy and Isabel by Michael Rosen
Collector of Moments by Quint Buchholz
Drylongso by Virginia Hamilton
Flags by Maxine Trottier
Josepha: A Prairie Boy's Story by Jim McGugan
Just Like New by Ainslie Manson
Nadia's Hands by Karen English
Nobiah's Well by Donna Guthrie
The Orphan Boy by Tololwa M. Mollel
Smoky Night by Eve Bunting
Tomás and the Library Lady by Pat Mora

Chapter Books
Almost a Hero by John Neufeld
All Alone in the Universe by Lynne Rae Perkins
Angel Square by Brian Doyle
The Apprenticeship of Lucas Whitaker by Cynthia DeFelice
Because of Winn-Dixie by Kate DiCamillo
Belle Prater's Boy by Ruth White
Bloomability by Sharon Creech
Bridge to Terabithia by Katherine Paterson
The Cay by Theodore Taylor
The Champion by Maurice Gee
Crash by Jerry Spinelli
Dear Mr. Sprouts by Errol Broome
Freak the Mighty by Rodman Philbrick
The Friendship by Mildred Taylor
The Gold Cadillac by Mildred Taylor
Harper and Moon by Ramon Royal Ross
Here's to You, Rachel Robinson by Judy Blume
Holes by Louis Sachar
Incident at Hawk's Hill by Allan W. Eckert
Jazmin's Notebook by Nikki Grimes

Lily's Crossing by Patricia Reilly Giff
The Maze by Will Hobbs
Next-Door Neighbors by Sarah Ellis
The Pool Party by Gary Soto
Return to Hawk's Hill by Allan W. Eckert
The Secret Life of Amanda K. Woods by Ann Cameron
Seedfolks by Paul Fleischman
The Sky is Falling by Kit Pearson
Spying on Miss Müller by Eve Bunting
Summer of the Mad Monk by Cora Taylor
Timothy of the Cay by Theodore Taylor
Tuck Everlasting by Natalie Babbit
The View from Saturday by E. L. Konigsberg
What Happened on Planet Kid by Jane Leslie Conly
Words of Stone by Kevin Henkes
When Zachary Beaver Came to Town by Kimberly Willis Holt

Young Adult
Alida's Song by Gary Paulsen
Arly by Robert Newton Peck
Bad Girls by Cynthia Voigt
Bat 6 by Virginia Euwer Wolff
Crazy Weekend by Gary Soto
Dangerous Skies by Suzanne Fisher Staples
The Exchange Student by Kae Gilmore
Go and Come Back by Joan Abelove
The Goats by Brock Cole
Heart of a Champion by Carl Deuker
Ironman by Chris Crutcher
Joyride by Gretchen Olson
Kissing Tennessee by Kathi Appelt
Letters from the Inside by John Marsden
Letters to Julia by Barbara Ware Holmes
Lord of the Fries and Other Stories by Tim Wynne Jones
The Maestro by Tim Wynne-Jones
Make Lemonade by Virginia Euwer Wolff
Music from a Place Called Half Moon by Jerrie Oughton
The Ornament Tree by Jean Thesman
Phoenix Rising by Karen Hesse
Revolutions of the Heart by Marsha Qualey
Slot Machine by Chris Lynch
Stargirl by Jerry Spinelli
Staying Fat for Sarah Byrnes by Chris Crutcher
Tears of a Tiger by Sharon Draper
Two Suns in the Sky by Miriam Bat-Ami
The Wild Children by Felice Holman
The Wish by Gail Carson Levine

Theme 2. Family Issues

Picture Books for Older Readers
The Bat Boy and His Violin by Gavin Curtis
Dandelions by Eve Bunting

Ma Dear's Aprons by Patricia McKissack
My Ol' Man by Patricia Polacco
My Rotten Redheaded Brother by Patricia Polacco
Tea with Milk by Allen Say
What You Know First by Patricia MacLachlan
Your Move by Eve Bunting

Chapter Books
Baby by Patricia MacLachlan
The Ballad of Lucy Whipple by Karen Cushman
Belle Prater's Boy by Ruth White
The Best Bad Thing by Yoshiko Uchida
The Birthday Room by Kevin Henkes
Breakaway by Paul Yee
Bud, Not Buddy by Christopher Paul Curtis
Chasing Redbird by Sharon Creech
Child of the Owl by Laurence Yep
Comfort Creek by Joyce McDonald
Cousins by Virginia Hamilton
Crazy Lady! by Leslie Jane Conly
The Crystal Drop by Monica Hughes
Discovering One Thing I'm Good At by Karen Lynn Williams
The Falcon's Wing by Dawna Lisa Buchanan
A Family Apart by Joan Lowery Nixon (series)
Family Tree by Katherine Ayres
Flying Solo by Ralph Fletcher
Getting Near to Baby by Audrey Coloumbis
The Great Gilly Hopkins by Katherine Paterson
Harper and Moon by Ramon Royal Ross
Hero of Lesser Causes by Julie Johnston
If Wishes Were Horses by Natalie Kinsey-Warnock
A Jar of Dreams by Yoshiko Uchida
Journey by Patricia MacLachlan
Mama, Let's Dance by Patricia Hermes
Mick Harte Was Here by Barbara Park
Missing May by Cynthia Rylant
Moving Mama to Town by Ronder Thomas Young
My Louisiana Sky by Kimberly Willis Holt
Nissa's Place by A. LaFaye
One Thing That's True by Cheryl Foggo
Our Only May Amelia by Jennifer Holm
Park's Quest by Katherine Paterson
Preacher's Boy by Katherine Paterson
Promise Song by Linda Holeman
The Rain Catchers by Jean Thesman
Risk 'n Roses by Jan Slepian
Sarah and Me and the Lady from the Sea by Patricia Beatty
Soldier Mom by Alice Mead
Someone to Count On by Patricia Hermes
Song of the Trees by Mildred Taylor
The Star Fisher by Laurence Yep

The Stone-Faced Boy by Paula Fox
Toning the Sweep by Angela Johnson
Torn Away by James Heneghan
The Trading Game by Alfred Slote
Trout Summer by Jane Leslie Conly
Uncle Ronald by Brian Doyle
Walk Two Moons by Sharon Creech
Walks in Beauty by Hazel Krantz
The Wanderer by Sharon Creech
The Watsons Go to Birmingham—1963 by Christopher Paul Curtis
Words of Stone by Kevin Henkes
The Year of the Sawdust Man by A. LaFaye
Yolonda's Genius by Carol Fenner

Young Adult
Among the Volcanos by Omar Castaneda
The Barn by Avi
Being with Henry by Martha Brooks
Bone Dance by Martha Brooks
California Blue by David Klass
Catherine, Called Birdy by Karen Cushman
Dave at Night by Gail Carson Levine
A Door Near Here by Heather Quarles
Dragon's Gate by Laurence Yep
Dragonwings by Laurence Yep
The Eagle's Shadow by Nora Martin
Earthshine by Theresa Nelson
Gideon's People by Carolyn Meyer
The Glory Field by Walter Dean Myers
Habibi by Naomi Shihab Nye
Hannah In Between by Colby Rodowsky
Heaven by Angela Johnson
Homecoming by Cynthia Voigt
Ironman by Chris Crutcher
The Islander by Cynthia Rylant
Jacob Have I Loved by Katherine Paterson
Journey of the Sparrows by Fran Leeper Buss with Daisy Cubias
Letters from Rifka by Karen Hesse
Like Sisters on the Home Front by Rita Williams-Garcia
A Lion to Guard Us by Clyde Robert Bulla
Listening for Leroy by Betsy Hearne
A Long Way from Chicago by Richard Peck
Make Lemonade by Virginia Euwer Wolff
Memoirs of a Bookbat by Kathryn Lasky
The One-Eyed Cat by Paula Fox
The Outsiders by S. E. Hinton
A Place to Call Home by Jackie French Koller
Probably Still Nick Swansen by Virginia Euwer Wolff
Shabanu: Daughter of the Wind by Suzanne Fisher Staples
Somewhere in the Darkness by Walter Dean Myers
Song of the Buffalo Boy by Sherry Garland

Sharla by Budge Wilson
Spite Fences by Trudy Krisher
Tribute to Another Dead Rock Star by Randy Powell
The True Colors of Caitlynne Jackson by Carol Lynch Williams
What Jamie Saw by Carolyn Coman
The Window by Michael Dorris
A Woman of Her Tribe by Margaret Robinson

Theme 3. Generations Learning from One Another

Picture Books for Older Readers
The Day GoGo Went to Vote by Elinor Betezat Sisulu
Grandfather's Journey by Allen Say
The Keeping Quilt by Patricia Polacco
Lucy's Picture by Nicola Moon
Luka's Quilt by Georgia Guback
The Memory Box by Mary Bahr
Muskrat Will Be Swimming by Cheryl Savageau
The Night the Grandfathers Danced by Linda Theresa Raczek
The Patchwork Quilt by Valerie Flournoy
The Remembering Box by Eth Clifford
The Summer My Father Was Ten by Pat Brisson
Sunshine Home by Eve Bunting
Three Cheers for Catherine the Great! by Cari Best
The Unbreakable Code by Sarah Hoagland Hunter
A Walk to the Great Mystery by Virginia Stroud
The Wall by Eve Bunting
Where is Grandpa? By T. A. Barron
The Year of Fire by Teddy Jam

Chapter Books
Alida's Song by Gary Paulsen
Anne of Green Gables by Lucy Maud Montgomery
The Eternal Spring of Mr. Ito by Sheila Garrigue
Jericho by Janet Hickman
Leaving Emma by Nancy Steele Brokaw
The Maze by Will Hobbs
Winter Camp by Kirkpatrick Hill

Young Adult
The Borning Room by Paul Fleischman
A Long Way from Chicago by Richard Peck
Mind's Eye by Paul Fleischman

Theme 4a. Challenges (Pursuing a Dream)

Picture Books for Older Readers
A Band of Angels by Deborah Hopkinson
Bill Pickett: Rodeo-Ridin' Cowboy by Andrea Davis Pinkney
El Chino by Allen Say
The Day GoGo Went to Vote by Elinor Betezat Sisulu
If I Only Had a Horn: Young Louis Armstrong by Roxanne Orgill
Jingle Dancer by Cynthia Leitich Smith
My Dream of Martin Luther King by Faith Ringgold

My Rows and Piles of Coins by Tololwa M. Mollel
Richard Wright and the Library Card by William Miller
Uncle Jed's Barbershop by Margaree King Mitchell

Easy Chapter Book
The Skates of Uncle Richard by Carol Fenner

Chapter Books
Building a Dream: Mary Bethune's School by Richard Kelso
I Have a Dream: The Story of Martin Luther King, Jr. by Margaret Davidson
Outward Dreams: Black Inventors and their Inventions by Jim Haskins
Trumpet of the Swan by E. B. White

Young Adult
Among the Volcanoes by Omar Castaneda
Dear Great American Writers School by Sherry Bunin
Dragonwings by Laurence Yep
Ironman by Chris Crutcher
The Mozart Season by Virginia Euwer Wolff
Unfinished Dreams by Jane Breskin Zalben

Theme 4b. Challenges (Taking Action to Care for Others)

Picture Books for Older Readers
Birdie's Lighthouse by Deborah Hopkinson
Garbage Creek and Other Stories by W. D. Valgardson

Chapter Books
Beardance by Will Hobbs
Bearstone by Will Hobbs
Belle Prater's Boy by Ruth White
Bridge to Terabithia by Katherine Paterson
The Eternal Spring of Mr. Ito by Sheila Garrigue
Freak the Mighty by Rodman Philbrick
Running Out of Time by Margaret Peterson Haddix

Young Adult
The Bamboo Flute by Gary Disher
The Bomb by Theodore Taylor
Cracker Jackson by Betsy Byars
Don't You Dare Read This, Mrs. Dunphrey by Margaret Peterson Haddix
The Goats by Brock Cole
Goodnight Mr. Tom by Michele Magorian
Hiding Mr. McNulty by Bernice Rabe
Rose Daughter by Robin McKinley
Slot Machine by Chris Lynch
Staying Fat for Sarah Byrnes by Chris Crutcher

Theme 4c. Challenges (Persevering Despite Obstacles)

Picture Books for Older Readers
The Babe and I by David Adler
Black Whiteness: Admiral Byrd Alone in the Antarctic by Robert Burleigh
Home to Medicine Mountain by Chiori Santiago
I Have Heard of a Land by Joyce Carol Thomas
Cassie's Journey by Brett Harvey

Ghost Train by Paul Yee
Lights on the River by Jane Resh Thomas
The Lotus Seed by Sherry Garland
Through My Eyes by Ruby Bridges
Zora Hurston and the Chinaberry Tree by William Miller

Chapter Books
Adaline Falling Star by Mary Pope Osborne
The Ballad of Lucy Whipple by Karen Cushman
The Captain's Dog by Roland Smith
Ghost Canoe by Will Hobbs
The Haymeadow by Gary Paulsen
Jip: His Story by Katherine Paterson
Maniac Magee by Jerry Spinelli
Sarah, Also Known as Hannah by Lillian Hammer Ross
Treasures in the Dust by Tracey Potter

Young Adult
The Golden Compass by Philip Pullman
Haveli by Suzanne Fisher Staples
Make Lemonade by Virginia Euwer Wolff
Monster by Walter Dean Myers
Nell's Quilt by Susan Terris
Phoenix Rising by Karen Hesse
Shabanu: Daughter of the Wind by Suzanne Fisher Staples
The Midwife's Apprentice by Karen Cushman
Out of the Dust by Karen Hesse
Slam! by Walter Dean Myers
Somehow Tenderness Survives by Hazel Rochman

Theme 4d. Challenges (Accepting Responsibility)

Picture Book for Older Readers
Too Many Tamales by Gary Soto

Young Adult
The Giver by Lois Lowry
The Shadow Children by Stephen Schnur
Whirligig by Paul Fleischman

Theme 4e. Challenges (Dealing with Adversity)

Picture Books for Older Readers
Baseball Saved Us by Ken Mochizuki
Blue Jay in the Desert by Marlene Shigekawa
The Bracelet by Yoshiko Uchida
The Memory Coat by Elvira Woodruff

Chapter Books
Against the Storm by Gaye Hicyilmaz
Goodbye Vietnam by Gloria Whelan
Guests by Michael Dorris
Journey Home by Yoshiko Uchida
Journey to Topaz by Yoshiko Uchida
Kiss the Dust by Elizabeth Laird

Morning Girl by Michael Dorris
Nim and the War Effort by Milly Lee
Pickle Song by Barthe De Clements
Purely Rosie Pearl by Patricia Cochrane
Under the Hawthorne Tree by Marta Conlon-McKenna
Walker of Time by Helen Hughes Vick

Young Adult
The Baboon King by Anton Quintana
Grab Hands and Run by Frances Temple
Halinka by Mirjam Pressler
The Journal of Ben Uchida: Citizen 13559 Mirror Lake Internment Camp by Berry
    Denenberg
Lupita Manana by Patricia Beatty
Matilda Bone by Karen Cushman
Scorpions by Walter Dean Myers
The Wall by Elizabeth Lutzeier

Theme 4f. Challenges (Overcoming Personal Challenges)

Picture Books for Older Readers
Listen for the Bus: David's Story by Patricia McMahon
Sadako by Eleanor Coerr
Thank You, Mr. Falker by Patricia Polacco
A Train to Somewhere by Eve Bunting
When Jessie Came Across the Sea by Amy Hest

Chapter Books
Boy by Roald Dahl
Earthly Astonishments by Marthe Jocelyn
Hero of Lesser Causes by Julie Johnston
Joey Pigza Swallowed the Key by Jack Gantos
The King of Dragons by Carol Fenner
Mick Harte was Here by Barbara Park
Tangerine by Edward Bloor
See Ya, Simon by David Hill
Missing May by Cynthia Rylant
The Music of the Dolphins by Karen Hesse
Sees Behind Trees by Michael Dorris
Spider Sparrow by Dick King-Smith
The Stone-Faced Boy by Paula Fox

Young Adult
All Alone in the Universe by Lynne Rae Perkins
Dogsong by Gary Paulsen
Just Ella by Margaret Peterson Haddix
The Monument by Gary Paulsen
Peeling the Onion by Wendy Orr
Petey by Ben Mikaelsen
Plain City by Virginia Hamilton
Samir and Yonatan by Daniella Carmi
The Shadow Spinner by Susan Fletcher
Stuck in Neutral by Terry Trueman
A Summer to Die by Lois Lowry

Theme 4g. Challenges (Finding a Place to Belong)

Picture Books for Older Readers

The Boy Who Wanted a Family by Shirley Gordon
Onion Tears by Diana Kidd
Radio Man by Arthur Dorros

Chapter Books

Adam and Eve and Pinch Me by Julie Johnston
Afternoon of the Elves by Janet Taylor Lisle
Angel and Me and the Bayside Bombers by Mary Jane Auch
Between Two Worlds by Candice Ransom
Call Me Ruth by Marilyn Sachs
Flip Flop Girl by Katherine Paterson
New Kids in Town by Janet Bode
A Place Not Home by Eva Wiseman
Strawberry Hill by A. LaFaye
Thief of Hearts by Laurence Yep

Young Adult

Children of the River by Linda Crew
Dakota Dream by James Bennett
The Great Gilly Hopkins by Katherine Paterson
Voices from the Fields: Children of Migrant Farmers Tell Their Stories by S. Beth Atkin
Tiltawhirl John by Gary Paulsen

Theme 4h. Challenges (Homeless Children)

Picture Books

Fly Away Home by Eve Bunting

Chapter Books

Almost a Hero by John Neufeld
Cave Under the City by Harry Mazer
Chive by Shelly Barre
A Family Pose by Dean Hughes
Family Under the Bridge by Natalie Carlson
King of Dragons by Carol Fenner
The Leaves of October by Karen Akerman
The Loner by Ester Wier
Maniac Magee by Jerry Spinelli
Monkey Island by Paula Fox
Nowhere to Call Home by Cynthia DeFelice
Pick-up Sticks by Sarah Ellis
A Place to Call Home by Jackie French Koller
Randall's Wall by Carol Fenner
Slake's Limbo by Felice Holman
When the Road Ends by Jean Thesman

Young Adult

Asphalt Angels by Ineke Holtwijz
Carolina Crow Girl by Valerie Hobbs
Dicey's Song by Cynthia Voigt
Homecoming by Cynthia Voigt
The Wild Children by Felice Holman

Theme 4i. Challenges (Searching for Truth)

Chapter Book
Walk Two Moons by Sharon Creech

Young Adult
Briar Rose by Jane Yolen
Dangerous Skies by Suzanne Fisher Staples
Gathering Blue by Lois Lowry
The Giver by Lois Lowry
Memoirs of a Bookbat by Kathryn Lasky
Nothing but the Truth by Avi
Sang Spell by Phyllis Reynolds Naylor
Walker's Crossing by Phyllis Reynolds Naylor
The Wanderer by Sharon Creech

Theme 5. Courage

Picture Book
Dakota Dugout by Ann Turner

Picture Books for Older Readers
Aunt Harriet's Underground Railroad in the Sky by Faith Ringgold
The Boy Called Slow by Joseph Bruchac
Brave as a Mountain Lion by Ann Herbert Scott
Fa Mulan: The Story of a Woman Warrior by Robert San Souci
Fire on the Mountain by Jane Kurtz
Gift Horse: A Lakota Story by S. D. Nelson
The Lily Cupboard by Shulamith Levey Oppenheim
Mirette on the High Wire by Emily Arnold McCully
One Yellow Daffodil by David Adler
A Promise is a Promise by Robert Munsch, Michael Kusugak, and Vladanya Krykorka
The Story of Ruby Bridges by Robert Coles
The Streets of Gold by Rosemary Wells
Sweet Clara and the Freedom Quilt by Deborah Hopkinson
Tales from Gold Mountain by Paul Yee
Through My Eyes by Ruby Bridges
Wilma Unlimited by Kathleen Krull

Chapter Books
Adrift by Alan Baillie
Climb or Die by Edward Myers
The Crystal Drop by Monica Hughes
A Dangerous Promise by Joan Lowery Nixon (series)
Echoes of the White Giraffe by Sook Nyul Choi
Incident at Hawk's Hill by Allan Eckert
I Rode A Horse of Milk White Jade by Diane Lee Wilson
Island of the Blue Dolphins by Scott O'Dell
Jericho's Journey by G. Clifton Wisler
Julie of the Wolves by Jean Craighead George
Night of the Twisters by Ivy Ruckman
Quake! A Novel by Joe Cottonwood

Rebel by Alan Baillie
Rescue Josh McGuire by Ben Mikaelsen
SOS Titanic by Eve Bunting
The Storyteller's Beads by Jane Kurtz
Thunder Cave by Roland Smith
Trouble's Daughter by Katherine Kirkpatrick
Troubling a Star by Madeleine L'Engle
Voyage of the Frog by Gary Paulsen
The Wanderer by Sharon Creech
Weasel by Cynthia DeFelice
Windcatcher by Avi
Woodsong by Gary Paulsen
A Wrinkle in Time by Madeleine L'Engle
Year of Impossible Goodbyes by Sook Nyul Choi

Young Adult
An Acquaintance with Darkness by Ann Rinaldi
Among the Hidden by Margaret Peterson Haddix
Anne Frank: Beyond the Diary by Ruud van der Rol and Rian Verhoeven
Beyond the Divide by Kathryn Lasky
Bull Run by Paul Fleischman
Burning Issy by Melvin Burgess
Cast Two Shadows by Ann Rinaldi
A Circle Unbroken by Sollace Hotze
Daniel's Story by Carol Matas
The Diary of Anne Frank by Anne Frank
Escape to the Forest by Ruth Yaffe Radin
The Fall of the Red Star by Helen Szablya and Peggy King Anderson
The Forty-Third War by Louise Moeri
Friedrich by Hans Peter Richter
Gathering Blue by Lois Lowry
The Hidden Children by Howard Greenfield
Homeless Bird by Gloria Whelan
In the Line of Fire: Eight Women War Spies by Irene Gut Opdyke
Jason's Gold by Will Hobbs
Legend Days by Jamake Highwater
Life and Death of Crazy Horse by Russell Freedman
Mine Eyes Have Seen by Ann Rinaldi
Nightjohn by Gary Paulsen
No Turning Back: A Novel of South Africa by Beverly Naidoo
One More River by Lynne Reid Banks
The Root Cellar by Janet Lunn
Sarny: A Life Remembered by Gary Paulsen
A Soldier's Heart by Gary Paulsen
Somehow Tenderness Survives by Hazel Rochman
Stones in Water by Donna Napoli
Ties that Bind, Ties that Break by Lensey Namioka
The Transall Saga by Gary Paulsen
Tusk and Stone by Malcolm Bosse
Undying Glory: The Story of the Massachusetts 54th Regiment by Clinton Cox

The Upstairs Room by Johanna Reiss
The Well of Sacrifice by Chris Eboch
With Every Drop of Blood by James Lincoln Collier and Christopher Collier

Theme 6. Standing Up for Your Beliefs

Picture Books for Older Readers

The Ballot Box Battle by Emily Arnold McCully
The Bobbin Girl by Emily Arnold McCully
A Boy Becomes a Man at Wounded Knee by Ted Wood
Crazy Horse's Vision by Joseph Bruchac
Dear Benjamin Banneker by Andrea Davis Pinkney
The Death of the Iron Horse by Paul Goble
Friends from the Other Side by Gloria Anzaldua
Ghandi by Leonard Everett Fisher
Ghost Dance by Alice McLerran
Granddaddy's Gift by Margaree King Mitchell
Harriet and the Promised Land by Jacob Lawrence
If a Bus Could Talk by Faith Ringgold
Joan of Arc by Diane Stanley
Leagues Apart: The Men and Times of the Negro Baseball Leagues by Lawrence Ritter
Mandela by Floyd Cooper
Minty: A Story of Young Harriet Tubman by Alan Schroeder
Molly Bannaky by Alice McGill
My Dream of Martin Luther King by Faith Ringgold
Now Let Me Fly: The Story of a Slave Family by Dolores Johnson
Passage to Freedom: The Sugihara Story by Ken Mochizuki
The People Who Hugged Trees by Deborah Lee Rose
She's Wearing a Dead Bird on Her Head by Kathryn Lasky
Sister Anne's Hands by Maribeth Lorbiecki
Starry Messenger by Peter Sis
Teammates by Peter Golenbock
White Socks Only by Evelyn Coleman

Chapter Books

Building a Dream: Mary Bethune's School by Richard Kelso
Chain of Fire by Beverly Naidoo
The Day the Women Got the Vote: A Photo History of the Women's Rights Movement by George Sullivan
Edwina Victorious by Susan Bonners
Francie by Karen English
Frindle by Andrew Clements
Ida B. Wells-Barnett: A Voice Against Violence by Patricia McKissack and Fredrick L. McKissack
Just Like Martin by Ossie Davis
Landry News by Andrew Clements
Lyddie by Katherine Paterson
Long Way to Go: A Story of Women's Right to Vote by Zibby Oneal
Making Waves by Barbara Williams
Marching to Freedom by Joyce Milton
Radical Red by Joyce Milton
Wringer by Jerry Spinelli

Young Adult
California Blue by David Klass
Catherine, Called Birdy by Karen Cushman
The Chocolate War by Robert Cormier
Ironman by Chris Crutcher
Lincoln: A Photobiography by Russell Freedman
Lockie Leonard, Scumbuster by Tim Winton
Memoirs of a Bookbat by Kathryn Lasky
Nightjohn by Gary Paulsen
Nothing But the Truth by Avi
Sarny: A Life Remembered by Gary Paulsen
Taste of Salt: A Story of Modern Haiti by Frances Temple
Ties that Bind, Ties that Break by Lensey Namioka
Unfinished Dreams by Jane Breskin Zalben
Warriors Don't Cry by Melba Patillo Beals
Witnesses to Freedom by Belinda Rochelle

Theme 7a. Justice

Picture Books
Satchel Paige by Lesa Cline-Ransome

Picture Books for Older Readers
Granddaddy's Gift by Margaree King Mitchell
In the Time of the Drums by Kim L. Siegelson
Nettie's Trip South by Ann Turner
Teammates by Peter Golenbock
Uncle Jed's Barbershop by Margaree King Mitchell
The Wagon by Tony Johnston
White Socks Only by Evelyn Coleman

Easy Chapter Books
Journey to Jo'burg by Beverly Naidoo
Mississippi Bridge by Mildred Taylor

Chapter Books
Amos Fortune: Free Man by Elizabeth Yates
Anthony Burns: The Defeat and Triumph of a Fugitive Slave by Virginia Hamilton
Breakaway by Paul Yee
Black Diamond: The Story of the Negro Baseball Leagues by Patricia McKissack and
    Fredrick L. McKissack, Jr.
Eleanor Roosevelt: Fighter for Social Justice by Ann Weil
Francie by Karen English
Hiding Mr. McNulty by Bernice Rabe
I Have a Dream: The Story of Martin Luther King by Margaret Davidson
Just Like Martin by Ossie Davis
Let the Circle Be Unbroken by Mildred Taylor
The Road to Memphis by Mildred Taylor
Roll of Thunder, Hear My Cry by Mildred Taylor
Sing Down the Moon by Scott O'Dell
Stealing Home: The Story of Jackie Robinson by Barry Denenberg
Thunder Rolling in the Mountains by Scott O'Dell and Elizabeth Hall
The Witch of Blackbird Pond by Elizabeth George Speare

Young Adult

Freedom Riders: Journey for Justice by James Haskins

Freedom's Children: Young Civil Rights Activists Tell Their Own Stories by Ellen Levine

From Slave to Civil War Hero: The Life and Times of Robert Smalls by Michael Cooper

The House of Dies Drear by Virginia Hamilton

Kinship by Trudy Krisher

Malcolm X: By Any Means Necessary by Walter Dean Myers

Many Thousand Gone: African Americans from Slavery to Freedom by Virginia Hamilton

The March on Washington by James Haskins

Now Is Your Time! The African American Struggle for Freedom by Walter Dean Myers

Rebels Against Slavery by Patricia McKissack and Fredrick L. McKissack

Rising Voices: Writings of Young Native Americans edited by Arlene Hirschfelder and Beverly Singer

Spite Fences by Trudy Krisher

Theme 7b. Justice (Child Labor)

Picture Books for Older Readers

Bobbin Girl by Emily Arnold McCully

Easy Chapter Books

Fire at the Triangle Factory by Holly Littlefield

Chapter Books

Kids at Work: Lewis Hine and the Crusade Against Child Labor by Russell Freedman

Lyddie by Katherine Paterson

Theme 8. Survival

Chapter Books

All Alone by Claire Huchet Bishop

Beardance by Will Hobbs

Bearstone by Will Hobbs

Belinda's Hurricane by Elizabeth Winthrop

Brian's Winter by Gary Paulsen

The Broken Blade by William Durbin

Call It Courage by Armstrong Sperry

The Cay by Theodore Taylor

The Clay Marble by Minfong Ho

Climb or Die by Edward Myers

The Crystal Drop by Monica Hughes

Down the Yukon by Will Hobbs

Downriver by Will Hobbs

Far North by Will Hobbs

The Fear Place by Phyllis Reynolds Naylor

The Green Book by Jill Paton Walsh

Hatchet by Gary Paulsen

The Haymeadow by Gary Paulsen

Island of the Blue Dolphin by Scott O'Dell
Julie by Jean Craighead George
Kokopelli's Flute by Will Hobbs
Little Brother by Alan Baillie
Lone Wolf by Kristine L. Franklin
My Brother Sam is Dead by James Lincoln Collier and Christopher Collier
My Side of the Mountain by Jean Craighead George
On the Far Side of the Mountain by Jean Craighead George
A Place of Lions by Eric Campbell
River Rats by Carolyn Stevermer
Shipwreck at the Bottom of the Earth by Jennifer Armstrong
Thundercave by Roland Smith
Timothy of the Cay by Theodore Taylor
Toughboy and Sister by Kirkpatrick Hill
Troubling a Star by Madeleine L'Engle
The True Confessions of Charlotte Doyle by Avi
Voyage of the Frog by Gary Paulsen
The Wanderer by Sharon Creech
War Comes to Willy Freeman by James Lincoln Collier and Christopher Collier
Weasel by Cynthia DeFelice
Winter Camp by Kirkpatrick Hill

Young Adult
The Last Oasis by Sue Pace
Parallel Journeys by Eleanor Ayer, Helen Waterford, and Alfons Heck
The Perilous Journey of the Donner Party by Marian Calabro
Tomorrow When the War Began by John Marsden (series)
The Transall Saga by Gary Paulsen

Theme 9. Respecting Nature
[See also Intermediate]

Picture Books for Older Readers
Henry Hikes to Fitchburg by Donald B. Johnson
A River Ran Wild by Lynne Cherry
The Shaman's Apprentice: A Tale of the Amazon Rain Forest by Lynne Cherry and
    Mark Plotkin
Snowflake Bentley by Jacqueline Briggs Martin
Volcano: The Eruption and Healing of Mount St. Helens by Patricia Lauber

Chapter Books
Frightful's Mountain by Jean Craighead George
Lostman's River by Cynthia DeFelice
My Side of the Mountain by Jean Craighead George
The Other Side of the Mountain by Jean Craighead George
Sign of the Beaver by Elizabeth George Speare
The Talking Earth by Jean Craighead George

Theme 10. Caring for Animals
[See Intermediate]

Genres

[See also Intermediate]

Genre 1. Fiction

[No Book List]

Genre 2. Historical Fiction

[See Time Periods]

Genre 3a. Biography (Sports Heroes)

[See Intermediate]

Genre 3b. Biography (Imagining the Future: Aviators, Explorers, Inventors and Scientists)

[See Intermediate]

Genre 3c. Biography (Leaders and Freedom Fighters)

Picture Books for Older Readers

Ghandi by Leonard Everett Fisher
Minty: A Story of Young Harriet Tubman by Alan Schroeder

Chapter Books

Anthony Burns: The Defeat and Triumph of a Fugitive Slave by Virginia Hamilton
In the Line of Fire: Eight Women War Spies by George Sullivan
Warriors Don't Cry by Melba Patillo Beals
Sojourner Truth: Ain't I A Woman? by Patricia McKissack and Frederick L. McKissack

Young Adult

Eleanor Roosevelt by Russell Freedman
Franklin Delano Roosevelt by Russell Freedman
Lincoln: A Photobiography by Russell Freedman

Genre 3d. Biography (Facing Challenges)

[See also Intermediate]

Picture Books for Older Readers

Bill Pickett: Rodeo Ridin' Cowboy by Andrea Davis Pinkney
Last Princess: The Story of Princess Kai'iulani of Hawaii by Fay Stanley
Vision of Beauty: The Story of Sarah Breedlove Walker by Kathryn Lasky

Chapter Books

At Her Majesty's Request: An African Princess in Victorian England by Walter Dean Myers
Homesick: My Own Story by Jean Fritz
The Invisible Thread by Yoshiko Uchida

Young Adult

Anne Frank: Beyond the Diary by Ruud van der Rol and Rian Verhoeven
Anne Frank: The Diary of a Young Girl by Anne Frank
Anne Frank: A Hidden Life by Mirjam Pressler
Red Scarf Girl: A Memoir of the Cultural Revolution by Ji Li Jiang
Where the Broken Heart Still Beats by Carolyn Meyer

Genre 3e. Biography (Artists, Musicians, Dancers, and Writers)

[See also Primary]

Picture Books
Alvin Ailey by Andrea Davis Pinkney
Charlie Parker Played Be Bop by Chris Raschka

Picture Books for Older Readers
Bard of Avon: The Story of William Shakespeare by Diane Stanley and Peter Vennema
Charles Dickens by Diane Stanley and Peter Vennema
Coming Home: From the Life of Langston Hughes by Quint Buchholz
Duke Ellington: The Piano Prince and his Orchestra by Andrea Davis Pinkney
If I Only Had a Horn: Young Louis Armstrong by Roxanne Orgill
Mysterious Thelonious by Chris Raschka
Satchmo's Blues by Alan Schroeder

Young Adult
Martha Graham: A Dancer's Life by Russell Freedman
Restless Spirit: The Life and Work of Dorothea Lange by Elizabeth Partridge

Genre 4. Mystery

[See Intermediate]

Genre 5. Fantasy

[See also Intermediate]

Chapter Books
Alanna by Tamora Pierce (series)
The Boggart by Susan Cooper
The Book of Three by Lloyd Alexander (series)
Bright Shadow by Avi
Clockwork by Philip Pullman
The Dark is Rising by Susan Cooper (series)
Dealing with Dragons by Patricia Wrede (series)
Dragon's Milk by Susan Fletcher (series)
Ella Enchanted by Gail Carson Levine
The Farthest Away Mountain by Lynne Reid Banks
The Fledgling by Jane Langton
The Forest Wife by Theresa Tomlinson
Half Magic by Edward Eager
The Half Men of O by Maurice Gee
Harry Potter and the Sorcerer's Stone by J. K. Rowling (series)
The Hobbit by J. R. R. Tolkien (series)
Honus & Me by Dan Gutman
I Am Mordred: A Tale from Camelot by Nancy Springer
In a Dark Wood by Michael Cadnum
The Iron Ring by Lloyd Alexander
The Lion Tamer's Daughter and Other Stories by Peter Dickinson
The Lion, the Witch, and the Wardrobe by C. S. Lewis (series)
Lost Magic by Berthe Amoss
The Lost Years of Merlin by T. A. Barron (series)
The Mennyms by Sylvia Waugh (series)
Merlin by Jane Yolen (series)
Midnight Magic by Avi
The Moorchild by Eloise McGraw
Mossflower by Brian Jacques (series)

Odder Than Ever by Bruce Coville
Owl in Love by Patricia Kindl
The Phantom Tollbooth by Norton Juster
Protector of the Small: First Test by Tamora Pierce (series)
Redwall by Brian Jacques (series)
Running Out of Time by Margaret Pederson Haddix
The Skull of Truth by Bruce Coville
Song Quest by Katherine Roberts
The Time Bike by Jane Langton
Tuck Everlasting by Natalie Babbitt

Young Adult
Firegold by Dia Calhoun
The Golden Compass by Philip Pullman (series)
The Queen of Attolia by Megan Whalen Turner
Sang Spell by Phyllis Reynolds Naylor
Sirena by Donna Jo Napoli
Walker of Time by Helen Hughes Vick

Genre 6. Science Fiction

Chapter Books
The Crystal Drop by Monica Hughes
The Green Book by Jill Paton Walsh
The Music of the Dolphins by Karen Hesse
Phoenix Rising by Karen Hesse
River Rats by Carolyn Stevermer
Starbright and the Dream Eater by Joy Cowley
The White Mountains by John Christopher (series)
A Wrinkle in Time by Madeleine L'Engle (series)

Young Adult
Among the Hidden by Margaret Pederson Haddix
The Ear, the Eye and the Arm by Nancy Farmer
The Exchange Student by Kate Gilmore
Gathering Blue by Lois Lowry
The Giver by Lois Lowry
The Last Oasis by Sue Pace
The Transall Saga by Gary Paulsen
Z for Zachariah by Robert C. O'Brien

Genre 7a. Traditional Literature
[See Intermediate]

Genre 7b. Traditional Literature (Twists on Fairy Tales)

Chapter Books
Book of Enchantments by Patricia Wrede
Crazy Jack by Donna Jo Napoli
Ella Enchanted by Gail Carson Levine
The Magic Circle by Donna Jo Napoli
Twelve Impossible Things Before Breakfast by Jane Yolen

Untold Tales by William Brooke (series)

A Wolf at the Door and Other Retold Fairy Tales edited by Ellen Datlow and Terri Windling

Zel by Donna Jo Napoli

Young Adult

Beauty by Robin McKinley

Just Ella by Margaret Pederson Haddix

Rose Daughter by Robin McKinley

Spindle's End by Robin McKinley

Spinners by Donna Jo Napoli

Genre 8. Nonfiction

[No Book List]

Genre 9. Poetry

Buried Alive: The Elements of Love by Ralph Fletcher

Dancing Teepees: Poems of American Indian Youth selected by Virginia Driving Hawk Sneve

Dreamkeeper and Other Poems by Langston Hughes

Fathers, Mothers, Sisters, Brothers: A Collection of Family Poems by Mary Ann Hoberman

Grand Mother: Poems, Reminiscences, and Short Stories about the Keepers of Our Tradition edited by Nikki Giovanni

I Am Wings: Poems about Love by Ralph Fletcher

I Feel a Little Jumpy around You by Naomi Shihab Nye and Paul Janezko

Navajo: Vision and Voices across the Mesa by Shonto Begay

Neighborhood Odes by Gary Soto

The Place My Words Are Looking For edited by Paul Janeczko

Rising Voices: Writings of Young Native Americans edited by Arlene Hirschfelder and Beverly Singer

Shimmy shimmy shimmy like my sister kate: Looking at Harlem through Renaissance Poems edited by Nikki Giovanni

Sports Pages by Arnold Adoff

Street Music: City Poems by Arnold Adoff

A Suitcase of Seaweed and Other Poems by Janet Wong

Time Periods

[See also Intermediate]

Time Period 1a. Looking into the Ancient Past

Picture Books

Beautiful Warrior: The Legend of the Nun's Kung Fu by Emily Arnold McCully

Picture Books for Older Readers

Fa Mulan: The Story of a Woman Warrior by Robert San Souci

Marco Polo: His Notebook by Susan Roth

Montezuma and the Fall of the Aztecs by Eric Kimmel

Sundiata: Lion King of Mali by David Wisniewski

Westward with Columbus by John Dyson

Chapter Books
I Columbus: My Journal 1492-1493 by Peter Roop and Connie Roop
I Sailed with Columbus by Miriam Schlein
Tainos: The People Who Welcomed Columbus by Francine Jacobs
The Trojan Horse: How the Greeks Won the War by Emily Little
Who Really Discovered America? by Stephen Krensky

Young Adult
Anna of Byzantium by Tracy Barret
The Bedouin's Gazelle by Frances Temple
I Rode a Horse of Milk White Jade by Diane Lee Wilson
Inside the Walls of Troy by Clemence McLaren
Tusk and Stone by Malcolm Bosse
Waiting for Odysseus by Clemence McLaren
The Well of Sacrifice by Chris Eboch

Time Period 1b. Looking into the Ancient Past (Egypt)

Picture Books for Older Readers
The Awesome Egyptians by Terry Deary and Peter Hepplewhite
Cleopatra by Diane Stanley and Peter Vennema
Egyptian Echo by Paul Dowsell
Egyptian Life by John Guy
The Egyptian News by Anton Powell and Philip Steele

Chapter Books
Cleopatra VII: Daughter of the Nile by Kristiana Gregory (The Royal Diaries series)

Young Adult
Mara, Daughter of the Nile by Eloise McGraw
Pharaoh's Daughter by Julius Lester

Time Period 2. Middle Ages and Renaissance

Picture Books for Older Readers
Bard of Avon: The Story of William Shakespeare by Diane Stanley and Peter Vennema
Good Queen Bess by Diane Stanley and Peter Vennema
Joan of Arc by Diane Stanley
The King's Fool: A Book about Medieval and Renaissance Fools by Dana Fradon
William Shakespeare's Macbeth retold by Bruce Coville (series)

Chapter Books
King of Shadows by Susan Cooper
A Lion to Guard Us by Clyde Robert Bulla
Outrageous Women of the Middle Ages by Vicki Leon
The Shakespeare Stealer by Gary Blackwood
The Whipping Boy by Sid Fleischman

Young Adult
The Burning Time by Carol Matas
Catherine, Called Birdy by Karen Cushman
Mary, Bloody Mary by Caroline Myer
Matilda Bone by Karen Cushman
The Midwife's Apprentice by Karen Cushman
Nell of Branford Hall by William Wise
The Ramsay Scallop by Frances Temple

Shadow Spinner by Susan Fletcher
The Stronghold by Mollie Hunter

Time Period 3a. Early Colonial (Issues of Slavery and Justice)

Picture Books for Older Readers
Dear Benjamin Banneker by Andrea Davis Pinkney
Molly Bannaky by Alice McGill

Chapter Books
Amos Fortune, Free Man by Elizabeth Yates
Jump Ship to Freedom by James Lincoln Collier and Christopher Collier
My Name is Not Angelica by Scott O'Dell
Slave Dancer by Paula Fox

Time Period 3b. Early Colonial (Salem Witch Trials)

Chapter Books
Tituba of Salem Village by Ann Petry
The Witch of Blackbird Pond by Elizabeth George Speare

Young Adult
Beyond the Burning Time by Kathryn Lasky
Burning Issy by Melvin Burgess

Time Period 4. Revolutionary War
[See also Intermediate]

Young Adult
Cast Two Shadows by Ann Rinaldi
Mine Eyes Have Seen by Ann Rinaldi

Time Period 5. Immigration and New Beginnings
[See also Intermediate]

Picture Books
Pepe the Lamplighter by Elisa Bartone

Picture Books for Older Readers
Ghost Train by Paul Yee
Grandfather's Journey by Allan Say
Journey to Ellis Island by Carol Bierman
The Keeping Quilt by Patricia Polacco
The Memory Coat by Elvira Woodruff
The Streets of Gold by Rosemary Wells
When Jessie Came Across the Sea by Amy Hest

Chapter Books
Beyond the Western Sea by Avi
Dragon's Gate by Laurence Yep
Dragonwings by Laurence Yep

Time Period 6. Westward Expansion (Multiple Perspectives)

Picture Books for Older Readers
Black Cowboys, Wild Horses: A True Story by Julius Lester
A Boy Called Slow by Joseph Bruchac
Cassie's Journey by Brett Harvey

Cheyenne Again by Eve Bunting
Crazy Horse's Vision by Joseph Bruchac
Daily Life in a Covered Wagon by Paul Erickson
Dandelions by Eve Bunting
Ghost Dance by Alice McLerran
Gift Horse by S. D. Nelson
Josepha: A Prairie Boy's Story by Jim McGugan
Laura's Album by William Anderson
My Prairie Year by Brett Harvey
Orphan Train Rider by Andrea Warren
Prairie Visions: The Life and Times of Soloman Butcher by Pam Conrad
Rachel's Journal by Marissa Moss
Train to Somewhere by Eve Bunting
West by Covered Wagon by Dorothy Hinshaw Patent

Chapter Books
Beyond the Divide by Kathryn Lasky
Children of the Wild West by Russell Freedman
Legend Days by Jamake Highwater
Sacajawea: The Story of Bird Woman and the Lewis and Clark Expedition by Joseph
    Bruchac

Young Adult
A Circle Unbroken by Sollace Hotze
Sweetgrass by Jan Hudson

Time Period 7. Slavery and the American Civil War

Picture Books for Older Readers
Aunt Harriet's Underground Railroad in the Sky by Faith Ringgold
Civil War Artist by Taylor Morrison
Harriet and the Promised Land by Jacob Lawrence
In the Time of the Drums by Kim L. Siegelson
Minty: A Story of Young Harriet Tubman by Alan Schroeder
More Than Anything Else by Marie Bradby
Nettie's Trip South by Ann Turner
Now Let Me Fly by Delores Johnson
Pink and Say by Patricia Polacco
Sweet Clara and the Freedom Quilt by Deborah Hopkinson
The Wagon by Tony Johnston

Chapter Books
Brady by Jean Fritz
Bull Run by Paul Fleishman
Cezanne Pinto by Mary Stolz
The Forgotten Heroes by Clinton Cox
Letters from a Slave Girl by Mary Lyons
The Long Road to Gettysburg by Jim Murphy
Rebels against Slavery by Patricia McKissack and Fredrick L. McKissack
A Separate Battle by Ina Chang

Young Adult
An Acquaintance with Darkness by Ann Rinaldi
The Boys' War: Confederate and Union Soldiers Talk about the War by Jim Murphy

Moon Over Tennessee: A Boy's Civil War Journal by Craig Crist-Evans
Nightjohn by Gary Paulsen
The Root Cellar by Janet Lunn
Sarny: A Life Remembered by Gary Paulsen
Soldier's Heart by Gary Paulsen
To Be a Slave by Julius Lester
Undying Glory by Clinton Cox
With Every Drop of Blood by James Lincoln Collier and Christopher Collier

Time Period 8. Gold Rush

Chapter Books
Alice Rose and Sam by Kathryn Lasky
The Ballad of Lucy Whipple by Karen Cushman
The Bite of the Gold Bug by Barthe DeClements
Bonanza Girl by Patricia Beatty
Down the Yukon by Will Hobbs
Dragon's Gate by Laurence Yep
Dragonwings by Laurence Yep
Gold Rush Women by Claire Rudolf Murphy and Jane Haigh
Tales from Gold Mountain by Paul Yee
Yukon Gold: The Story of the Klondike Gold Rush by Charlotte Foltz Jones

Young Adult
Jason's Gold by Will Hobbs

Time Period 9. Turn of the Century

[See also Intermediate]

Picture Books
Mailing May by Michael Tunnell
Marven of the Great North Woods by Kathryn Lasky

Picture Books for Older Readers
Coming Home: From the Life of Langston Hughes by Floyd Cooper
The Glorious Flight by Alice Provensen and Martin Provensen
Mirette on the High Wire by Emily Arnold McCully
True Heart by Marissa Moss

Young Adult
Nell's Quilt by Susan Terris
The Ornament Tree by Jean Thesman
The Tree of Bells by Jean Thesman

Time Period 10. Women's Rights Movement

Picture Books
Bloomers! by Rhoda Blumberg

Picture Books for Older Readers
The Ballot Box Battle by Emily Arnold McCully
The Bobbin Girl by Emily Arnold McCully
She's Wearing a Dead Bird on Her Head by Katherine Lasky

Chapter Books
The Day Women Got the Vote by George Sullivan
A Long Way to Go by Zibby Oneal

Radical Red by James Duffy
So, You Want Women to Vote, Lizzie Stanton? by Jean Fritz

Time Period 11. Great Depression

Picture Books for Older Readers
The Babe and I by David Adler
The Dust Bowl by David Booth
The Gardener by Sarah Stewart
Home to Medicine Mountain by Chiori Santiago
Uncle Jed's Barbershop by Margaree King Mitchell

Chapter Books
The Bamboo Flute by Gary Disher
The Barn Burner by Patricia Willis
Bud, Not Buddy by Christopher Paul Curtis
Children of the Dustbowl by Jerry Stanley
Dave at Night by Gail Carson Levine
Francie by Karen English
Hiding Mr. McNulty by Bernice Rabe
A Jar of Dreams by Yoshiko Uchida
Let the Circle Be Unbroken by Mildred Taylor
Nowhere to Call Home by Cynthia DeFelice
Roll of Thunder, Hear My Cry by Mildred Taylor
Song of the Trees by Mildred Taylor
Summer of the Mad Monk by Cora Taylor

Young Adult
Hiding Mr. McNulty by Bernice Rabe
Out of the Dust by Karen Hesse
Road to Memphis by Mildred Taylor

Time Period 12a. World War II

Picture Books for Older Readers
The Bicycle Man by Allan Say
Faithful Elephants by Yukio Tsuchiya
Just Like New by Ainslie Manson
Sadako by Eleanor Coerr

Easy Chapter Books
Sadako and the Thousand Paper Cranes by Eleanor Coerr

Chapter Books
Angel Square by Brian Doyle
Autumn Street by Lois Lowry
Bat 6 by Virginia Euwer Wolff
Behind the Bedroom Wall by Laura Williams
Cassandra: Live at Carnegie Hall by Nancy Hopper
The Cay by Theodore Taylor
The Champion by Maurice Gee
Foster's War by Carolyn Reeder
Harper and Moon by Ramon Royal Ross
In the Line of Fire: Eight Women War Spies by George Sullivan
Lily's Crossing by Patricia Reilly Giff

Risk 'n Roses by Jan Slepian
The Sky is Falling by Kit Pearson
Snow Treasure by Marie McSwigan
Spying on Miss Müller by Eve Bunting
Stepping on the Cracks by Mary Downing Hahn
Timothy of the Cay by Theodore Taylor
When the Soldiers Were Gone by Vera W. Propp
Who Was That Masked Man, Anyway? by Avi

Young Adult
Briar Rose by Jane Yolen
Good Night, Mr. Tom by Michelle Magorian
Halinka by Mirjam Pressler
Paper Faces by Rachel Anderson

Time Period 12b. Holocaust

Picture Books for Older Readers
Hilde and Eli: Children of the Holocaust by David Adler
Let the Celebrations Begin! by Margaret Wild
The Lily Cupboard by Shulamith Oppenheim
One Yellow Daffodil by David Adler
Passage to Freedom: The Sugihara Story by Ken Mochizuki
The Picture Book of Anne Frank by David Adler
Rose Blanche by Roberto Innocenti and Christopher Gallaz

Chapter Books
Behind the Secret Window by Nellie Toll
The Big Lie by Isabella Leitner
Daniel's Story by Carol Matas
The Good Liar by Gregory Maguire
The Hidden Children by Howard Greenfield
Hide and Seek by Ida Vos
The Journey Back by Johanna Reiss
Kris's War by Carol Matas
The Night Crossing by Karen Ackerman
Number the Stars by Lois Lowry
So Young to Die: The Story of Hannah Senesh by Candice Ransom
Twenty and Ten by Claire Huchet Bishop

Young Adult
Anne Frank: Beyond the Diary by Ruud van der Rol and Rian Verhoeven
Anne Frank: The Diary of a Young Girl by Anne Frank
The Devil's Arithmetic by Jane Yolen
Escape to the Forest by Ruth Yaffe Radin
Friedrich by Hans Peter Richter
I Have Lived a Thousand Years by Livia Bitton-Jackson
In My Hands: Memories of a Holocaust Survivor by Irene Gut Opdyke
Never to Forget: The Jews of the Holocaust by Milton Meltzer
Parallel Journeys by Eleanor Ayer, Helen Waterford, and Alfons Heck
The Shadow Children by Steven Schnur
Stones in Water by Donna Jo Napoli
Tell Them We Remember: The Story of the Holocaust by Susan Bachrach
Torn Thread by Anne Isaacs

Upon the Head of the Goat by Aranka Siegal
The Upstairs Room by Johanna Reiss
We Remember the Holocaust by David Adler

Time Period 13. Japanese Internment

Picture Books for Older Readers
Baseball Saved Us by Ken Mochizuki
Blue Jay in the Desert by Marlene Shigekawa
The Bracelet by Yoshiko Uchida
Flags by Maxine Trottier
So Far From the Sea by Eve Bunting

Chapter Books
Children of the Relocation Camps by Catherine Welch
The Children of Topaz by Michael O. Tunnell and George W. Chilcoat
The Eternal Spring of Mr. Ito by Sheila Garrigue
Farewell to Manizar by Jeanne Wakatsuki and James Houston
I Am an American by Jerry Stanley
The Invisible Thread by Yoshiko Uchida
The Journal of Ben Uchida: Citizen 13559 Mirror Lake Internment Camp by Barry Denenberg
Journey Home by Yoshiko Uchida
Journey to Topaz by Yoshiko Uchida
The Moved-Outers by Florence Crannell Means
Naomi's Road by Joy Kogana
Nim and the War Effort by Milly Lee
Under the Blood Red Sun by Graham Salisbury

Time Period 14. Civil Rights Movement
[See also Intermediate]

Picture Books for Older Readers
Granddaddy's Gift by Margaree King Mitchell
If a Bus Could Talk by Faith Ringgold
My Dream of Martin Luther King, Jr. by Faith Ringgold
National Civil Rights Museum Celebrates Everyday People by Alice Faye Dunkin
The Story of Ruby Bridges by Robert Coles
Teammates by Peter Golenbock
Through My Eyes by Ruby Bridges

Easy Chapter Books
Mississippi Bridge by Mildred Taylor

Chapter Books
The Day Martin Luther King Jr. Was Shot by Jim Haskins
Freedom's Children by Ellen Levine
Freedom Riders by James Haskins
I Have a Dream by Margaret Davidson
Just Like Martin by Ossie Davis
Listening for Leroy by Betsy Hearne
The March on Washington by Jim Haskins
Marching to Freedom by Joyce Milton
The Watsons Go to Birmingham—1963 by Christopher Paul Curtis

Witnesses to Freedom by Belinda Rochelle

Young Adult
Kinship by Trudy Krisher
Leon's Story by Leon Tillage
Malcolm X: By Any Means Necessary by Walter Dean Myers
Spite Fences by Trudy Krisher
White Lilacs by Carolyn Meyer

Time Period 15. Conflict in Vietnam and Southeast Asia

Picture Books for Older Readers
The Lotus Seed by Sherry Garland
The Wall by Eve Bunting

Easy Chapter Books
The Wall of Names by Judy Donnelly

Chapter Books
Always Remember: The Story of the Vietnam Veteran's Memorial by Brent Ashabranner
The Clay Marble by Minfong Ho
Goodbye Vietnam by Gloria Whelan
Little Brother by Alan Baillie
Onion Tears by Diana Kidd
Park's Quest by Katherine Paterson
Song of the Buffalo Boy by Sherry Garland

Young Adult
Children of the River by Linda Crew

Time Period 16a. Contemporary Challenges in Other Countries

Young Adult
The Fall of the Red Star by Helen Szablya and Peggy King Anderson (Hungary)
The Forty-Third War by Louise Moeri (Central America)
A Girl Named Disaster by Nancy Farmer (Mozambique and Zimbabwe)
Go and Come Back by Joan Abelove (Peru)
Grab Hands and Run by Frances Temple (El Salvador)
Habibi by Naomi Shihab Nye (Israel)
Haveli by Suzanne Fisher Staples (Pakistan)
Homeless Bird by Gloria Wheelan (India)
Journey of the Sparrows by Fran Leeper Buss with Daisy Cubias (El Salvador)
Kiss the Dust by Elizabeth Laird (Iraq)
One More River by Lynn Reid Banks (Israel)
Red-Scarf Girl: A Memoir of the Cultural Revolution by Ji Li Jiang (China)
The Road from Home: The Story of an Armenian Girl by David Kherdian (Armenia)
Samir and Yonatan by Daniella Carmi (Israel)
Shabanu: Daughter of the Wind by Suzanne Fisher Staples (Pakistan)
Shiva's Fire by Suzanne Fisher Staples (India)
A Taste of Salt: A Tale of Modern Haiti by Frances Temple (Haiti)
Ties that Bind, Ties that Break by Lensey Namioka (China)
The Voices of Silence by Bel Mooney (Romania)
The Wall by Elizabeth Lutzeier (Germany)
Zlata's Diary: A Child's Life in Sarajevo by Zlata Filipovic (Yugoslavia)

Time Period 16b. Contemporary Challenges in Other Countries (Africa)
[See also Intermediate]

Picture Books for Older Readers
The Day GoGo Went to Vote by Elinor Betezat Sisulu
Mandela by Floyd Cooper

Easy Chapter Books
Journey to Jo'burg by Beverly Naidoo

Chapter Books
Chain of Fire by Beverly Naidoo
Somehow Tenderness Survives: Stories of Southern Africa by Hazel Rochman
The Storyteller's Beads by Jane Kurtz
Thunder Cave by Roland Smith

Young Adult
No Turning Back: A Novel of South Africa by Beverly Naidoo
Waiting for the Rain by Sheila Gordon

Part 4

Sample Author Studies

Primary

Jan Brett

Armadillo Rodeo
Berlioz the Bear
The Hat
The Mitten

Eve Bunting

A Day's Work
Fly Away Home
Smoky Night
Sunshine Home
The Wednesday Surprise

Joanna Cole and Bruce Degan

The Magic Schoolbus series

Tomie de Paola
(Generations Learning from One Another)

26 Fairmount Avenue
Here We All Are
Nana Upstairs, Nana Downstairs
Now One Foot, Now the Other
Tom

Mem Fox

Koala Lou
Possum Magic
Wilfrid Gordon McDonald Partridge

Kevin Henkes

Chester's Way
Chrysanthemum
Julius, Baby of the World
Lilly's Purple Plastic Purse
Owen
Sheila Rae, the Brave

Steven Kellogg (Tall Tales)

Johnny Appleseed
Mike Fink

Paul Bunyan
Pecos Bill
Sally Ann Thunder Ann Whirlwind Crockett

Leo Lionni

Frederick
Matthew's Dream
Swimmy

Gerald McDermott
(Traditional Literature)

Anansi the Spider
Arrow to the Sun
Coyote
Papagayo
Raven
Zomo the Rabbit

William Steig

The Amazing Bone
Amos and Boris
Caleb & Kate
Doctor DeSoto
Sylvester and the Magic Pebble

Chris Van Allsburg

Bad Day at Riverbend
The Garden of Abdul Gasazi
Jumanji
Just a Dream
The Mysteries of Harris Burdick
The Sweetest Fig
The Wretched Stone

Vera B. Williams

A Chair for My Mother
Cherries and Cherry Pits
Something Special for Me
Stringbean's Trip to the Shining Sea

Intermediate Grades

Karen Hesse

Just Juice
Letters from Rifka
The Music of Dolphins
Out of the Dust
Phoenix Rising
Sable

Katherine Paterson

Bridge to Terabithia
Flip-Flop Girl
The Great Gilly Hopkins
Jip: His Story
Lyddie
Park's Quest
Preacher's Boy

Gary Paulsen

Brian's Winter

Harris and Me
Hatchet
Haymeadow
The River
Voyage of the Frog
Woodsong

Patricia Polacco

The Bee Tree
Chicken Sunday
Just Plain Fancy
Mrs. Katz and Tush
The Keeping Quilt
My Ol'Man
My Rotten Redheaded Older Brother
Pink and Say
Thank You, Mr. Falker
Thundercake
Tikvah Means Hope

Upper Intermediate/Middle School

Paul Fleischman

The Borning Room
Bull Run
Mind's Eye
Saturnalia
Seedfolks
Whirligig

Karen Hesse

Letters from Rifka
The Music of the Dolphins
Out of the Dust
Phoenix Rising
A Time of Angels

Will Hobbs

Beardance
Bearstone
The Big Wander
Down the Yukon
Far North
Ghost Canoe

Jason's Gold
Kokopelli's Flute
The Maze

Walter Dean Myers

145th Street: Short Stories
At Her Majesty's Request
Malcolm X: By Any Means Necessary
Monster
Scorpions
Slam!
Somewhere in the Darkness

Gary Paulsen

Alida's Song
Dogsong
The Monument
Nightjohn
Sarny: A Life Remembered
Soldier's Heart
Tiltawhirl John
Transall Saga

Meet the Author Collection from Richard C. Owen Publishers

Biographies of well-known authors and illustrators revealing information about their childhood, their writing/illustrating process, and interesting facts about their work.

Verna Aardema	Karla Kuskin
David Adler	Jonathan Locker
Frank Asch	Jonathan London
Joseph Bruchac	George Ella Lyon
Eve Bunting	Margaret Mahy
Lynne Cherry	Rafe Martin
Lois Ehlert	Patricia McKissak
Jean Fritz	Patricia Polacco
Paul Goble	Laurence Pringle
Ruth Heller	Cynthia Rylant
Lee Bennett Hopkins	Seymour Simon
James Howe	Jean Van Leeuween
Johanna Hurwitz	Jane Yolen

Books about Authors/Illustrators

Andronik, Catherine M. (1993). *Kindred spirit: A biography of L. M. Montgomery, creator of Anne of Green Gables.* New York: Atheneum.

Blair, Gwenda. (1981). *Laura Ingalls Wilder.* New York: Putnam.

Bruce, Harry. (1992). *Maud: The life of L. M. Montgomery.* New York: Bantam.

Buchan, Elizabeth. (1987). *Beatrix Potter: The story of the creator of Peter Rabbit.* New York: Penguin.

Byars, Betsy. (1991). *The moon and I.* Englewood Cliffs, NJ: Julian Messner.

Campbell, Patricia. (1985). *Presenting Robert Cormier.* Boston: Twayne Publishers.

Carpenter, Angelica. (1990). *Frances Hodgson Burnett: Beyond The Secret Garden.* Minneapolis, MN: Lerner.

Cleary, Beverly. (1988). *A girl from Yamhill: A memoir.* New York: Dell.

Cleary, Beverly. (1995). *My own two feet: A memoir.* New York: Morrow.

Cole, Joanna, & Saul, Wendy. (1996). *On the bus with Joanna Cole: A creative autobiography.* Portsmouth, NH: Heinemann.

Collins, David. (1989). *Country artist: A story about Beatrix Potter.* Minneapolis, MN: Carolrhoda.

Collins, David. (1989). *To the point: A story about E. B. White.* Minneapolis, MN: Carolrhoda.

Copeland, Jeffrey. (1993). *Speaking of poets: Interviews with poets who write for children and young adults.* Urbana, IL: National Council of Teachers of English.

Copeland, Jeffrey, & Copeland, Vicky. (1994). *Speaking of poets 2: More interviews with poets who write for children and young adults.* Urbana, IL: National Council of Teachers of English.

Cummings, Pat. (Ed.). (1992). *Talking with artists.* New York: Bradbury.

Cummings, Pat. (Ed.). (1997). *Talking with artists 2.* New York: Clarion.

Cummings, Pat. (Ed.). (1999). *Talking with artists 3.* New York: Clarion.

Dahl, Roald. (1986). *Going solo.* New York: Viking Penguin.

Dahl, Roald. (1984). *Boy.* New York: Penguin.

Daly, John. (1989). *Presenting S. E. Hinton.* New York: Dell.

Duncan, Lois. (1982). *Chapters: My growth as a writer.* Boston: Little, Brown.

Dunkle, Margaret. (Ed.). (1987). *The story makers.* Melbourne, Australia: Oxford University Press.

Fleischman, Sid. (1996). *The abracadabra kid: A writer's life.* New York: Greenwillow.

Fox, Mem. (1992). *Dear Mem Fox, I have read all your books even the pathetic ones: And other incidents in the life of a children's book author.* San Diego, CA: Harcourt Brace Jovanovich.

Fox, Mem. (1993). *Radical reflections: Passionate opinions on teaching, learning, and living.* San Diego, CA: Harcourt Brace Jovanovich.

Fritz, Jean. (1982). *Homesick: My own story.* New York: Dell.

Gallo, Donald. (Ed.). (1990). *Speaking for ourselves: Autobiographical sketches by notable authors of books for young adults.* Urbana, IL: National Council of Teachers of English.

Gallo, Donald. (Ed.). (1992). *Authors' insights: Turning teenagers into readers and writers.* Portsmouth, NH: Heinemann.

Gallo, Donald. (Ed.). (1993). *Speaking for ourselves, too: More autobiographical sketches by notable authors of books for young adults.* Urbana, IL: National Council of Teachers of English.

Gherman, Beverly. (1992). *E. B. White: Some writer.* New York: Atheneum.

Greene, Carol. (1995). *Frances Hodgson Burnett: Author of The Secret Garden.* Chicago: Children's Press.

Greenwood, Barbara, & McKim, Audrey. (1987). *Her special vision: A biography of Jean Little.* Toronto: Irwin.

Hearne, Betsy. (Ed.). (1993). *The Zena Sutherland lectures 1983–1992.* New York: Clarion.

Hunter, Mollie. (1976). *Talent is not enough: Mollie Hunter on writing for children.* New York: Harper & Row.

Hurwitz, Johanna. (1989). *Astrid Lindgren: Storyteller to the world.* NY: Viking Penguin.

Hyman, Trina Schart. (1981). *Trina Schart Hyman: Self-portrait.* New York: Addison-Wesley.

Kiefer, Barbara. (Ed.). (1991). *Getting to know you: Profiles of children's authors featured in Language Arts 1985–1990.* Urbana, IL: National Council of Teachers of English.

Kovacs, Deborah, & Preller, James. (1991). *Meet the authors and illustrators: 60 creators of favorite children's books talk about their work.* New York: Scholastic.

Kovacs, Deborah & Preller, James. (1993). *Meet the authors and illustrators: 60 creators of favorite children's books talk about their work, volume two.* New York: Scholastic.

Lasky, Kathryn, & Knight, Maribah. (1993). *Searching for Laura Ingalls.* Photographs by Christopher G. Knight. New York: Macmillan.

Lee, Betsy. (1981). *Judy Blume's story.* New York: Dillon.

Little, Jean. (1987). *Little by Little: A writer's education.* New York: Penguin.

Little, Jean. (1990). *Stars come out within.* New York: Viking.

Lowry, Lois. (1998). *Looking back: A book of memories.* Boston: Houghton Mifflin.

Marcus, Leonard. (1991). *Margaret Wise Brown: Awakened by the moon.* Boston: Beacon Press.

Marcus, Leonard. (Ed.). (2000). *Author talk: Conversations with . . .* New York: Simon & Schuster.

Meltzer, Milton. (1988). *Starting from home: A writer's beginnings.* New York: Viking Penguin.

Naylor, Phyllis Reynolds. (1987). *How I came to be a writer.* New York: Macmillan.

Neimark, Anne. (1996). *Myth maker: J. R. R. Tolkien.* San Diego, CA: Harcourt.

Norby, Shirley & Ryan, Gregory. (1988). *Famous children's authors: Book one.* Minneapolis, MN: T. S. Denison.

Norby, Shirley & Ryan, Gregory. (1989). *Famous children's authors: Book two.* Minneapolis, MN: T. S. Denison.

Paterson, Katherine. (1981). *Gates of excellence: On reading and writing books for children.* New York: Dutton.

Paterson, Katherine. (1989). *The spying heart: More thoughts on reading and writing books for children.* New York: Dutton.

Peck, Richard. (1991). *Anonymously yours: A memoir.* Englewood Cliffs, NJ: Simon & Schuster.

Peet, Bill. (1989). *Bill Peet: An autobiography.* Boston: Houghton Mifflin.

Rylant, Cynthia. (1989). *But I'll be back again: An album.* New York: Orchard.

Soto, Gary. (1992). *Living up the street: Narrative recollections.* New York: Dell.

Spinelli, Jerry. (1998). *Knots in my yo-yo string: The autobiography of a kid.* New York: Knopf.

Taylor, Judy. (1988). *Beatrix Potter 1866–1943: The artist and her work.* New York: Warne.

Taylor, Judy. (1992). *Letters to children from Beatrix Potter.* New York: Warne.

Uchida, Yoshiko. (1992). *The invisible thread: A memoir by the author of The Best Bad Thing.* Englewood Cliffs, NJ: Messner.

Weidt, Maryann. (1989). *Presenting Judy Blume.* Boston: Twayne.

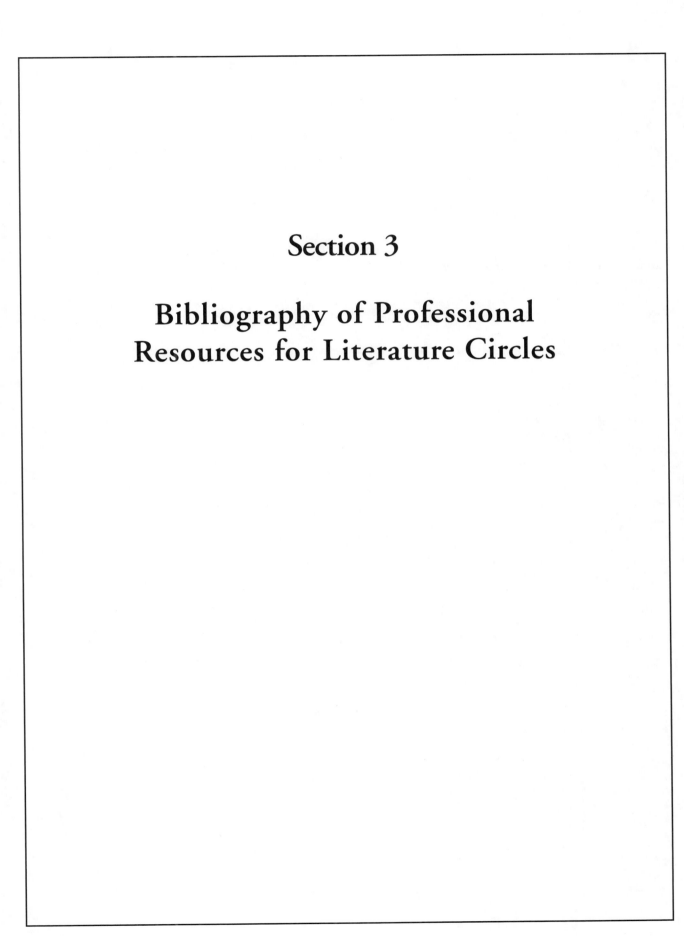

Section 3

Bibliography of Professional Resources for Literature Circles

Part 1

Professional Resources on Literature Circles and Response

Blecher, Sharon, & Jaffee, Kathy. (1998). *Weaving in the arts: Widening the learning circle*. Portsmouth, NH: Heinemann.

Daniels, Harvey. (1994). *Literature circles: Voice and choice in a student-centered classroom*. York, ME: Stenhouse.

Dodson, Shirley. (1997). *The mother-daughter book club*. New York: HarperCollins.

Hill, Bonnie, Ruptic, Cynthia, & Norwick, Lisa. (1998). *Classroom based assessment*. Norwood, MA: Christopher-Gordon.

Hill, Bonnie Campbell, Johnson, Nancy J., & Schlick Noe, Katherine L. (Eds.). (1995). *Literature circles and response*. Norwood, MA: Christopher-Gordon.

Holland, Kathleen, Hungerford, Rachael, & Ernst, Shirley. (1993). *Journeying: Children responding to literature*. Portsmouth, NH: Heinemann.

"Literature Circles: Growing Our Reading Lives," *Primary Voices*, Volume 9 (1), August, 2000 issue, Urbana, IL: NCTE.

Peterson, Ralph, & Eeds, Maryann. (1990). *Grand conversations: Literature groups in action*. New York: Scholastic.

Roser, Nancy, & Martinez, M. (Eds.). (1985). *Book talk and beyond: Children and teachers respond to literature*. Newark, DE: International Reading Association.

Routman, Regie. (2000). *Conversations: Strategies for teaching, learning, and evaluating*. Portsmouth, NH: Heinemann.

Routman, Regie. (1991, 1994). *Invitations: Changing as teachers and learners K–12*. Portsmouth, NH: Heinemann.

Samway, Katharine Davies, & Whang, Gail. (1995). *Literature study circles in a multicultural classroom*. York, ME: Stenhouse.

Schlick Noe, Katherine L., & Johnson, Nancy J. (1999). *Getting started with literature circles*. Norwood, MA: Christopher-Gordon.

Short, Kathy Gnagy, & Pierce, Kathryn Mitchell. (Eds.) (1990). *Talking about books: Creating literate communities*. Portsmouth, NH: Heinemann.

Strube, Penny. (1996). *Getting the most from literature groups*. New York: Scholastic.

Part 2

Professional Book Publishers

Christopher-Gordon Publishers: (800) 934-8322; (781) 762-5577

> http://www.christopher-gordon.com (under construction; operational spring 2000)

Heinemann Publishers: (800) 541-2086; (603) 431-7894

> http://www.heinemann.com

Irwin Publishers: (905) 660-0611

Richard C. Owens Publishers: (800) 336-5588

> http://www.rcowen.com

Stenhouse Publishers: (800) 988-9812; (207) 363-9198

> http://www.stenhouse.com

Part 3

Web Site Resources for Literature Circles

Literature Circles

Literature Circles Resource Center

http://fac-staff.seattleu.edu/kschlnoe/LitCircles/

LiteratureCircles.Com

http://www.literaturecircles.com

Children's Literature

Children's Literature Web Guide

http://www.acs.ucalgary.ca/~dkbrown/index.html

Carol Hurst's Children's Literature Site

http://www.carolhurst.com/

Teaching with Children's Literature

http://fac-staff.seattleu.edu/kschlnoe/ChildLit.html

Searchable Databases of Children's Literature

Database of Award-Winning Children's Literature

http://www2.wcoil.com/~ellerbee/childlit.html

Children's Picture Book Database at Miami University

http://www.lib.muohio.edu/pictbks/

About the Authors

From left to right: Bonnie Campbell Hill, Katherine L. Schlick Noe and Nancy J. Johnson

Bonnie Campbell Hill is a nationally and internationally known educational consultant in the areas of children's literature, writing, and assessment. She spent 10 years as a classroom teacher and continues to work closely with elementary students and teachers. Bonnie is co-editor, with Nancy J. Johnson and Katherine L. Schlick Noe, of *Literature Circles and Response*; co-author of *Practical Aspects of Authentic Assessment* with Cynthia Ruptic; and co-uthor of *Classroom Based Assessment* with Cynthia Ruptic and Lisa Norwick, all published by Christopher-Gordon.

Katherine L. Schlick Noe is Professor of Education and Coordinator of Reading at Seattle University. A former high school teacher, she received her Ph.D. in Reading/Language Arts from the University of Washington. Katherine is co-editor, with Bonnie Campbell Hill and Nancy J. Johnson, of *Literature Circles and Response*; and co-author of *Getting Started with Literature Circles* with Nancy J. Johnson, all published by Christopher-Gordon.

Nancy J. Johnson is a Professor in the English Department at Western Washington University. Prior to receiving her Ph.D. from Michigan State University, she taught 5th and 9th grades. Nancy is co-editor, with Bonnie Campbell Hill and Katherine L. Schlick Noe, of *Literature Circles and Response*; and co-author of *Getting Started with Literature Circles* with Katherine L. Schlick Noe, all published by Christopher-Gordon.